The World According to Michael excites a feeling of love and warmth and humor, not only within yourself but toward the others you have chosen to interact with in this lifetime. Guilt is released. A wonderful feeling of freedom comes in knowing who you are and why you have certain desires—or don't have them! Immensely clarifying. —Chris Adams

From the book:

To expect your Old Soul child to make a successful climb up some corporate ladder is unrealistic. Likewise, it's in error to expect an aggressive Young Soul attorney to turn her attention towards saving the environment; or to imagine a Mature Soul embroiled in some emotional drama would be able to calm down because you showed him the "big picture".

People who come into the Michael teaching are usually relieved to find out *why* they are different from mainstream society. They always knew it anyway. To get the explanation is helpful. It becomes easier to understand why it is that some share their global perspectives and others, no matter how intelligent, just aren't interested.

The World According To Michael

An Old Soul's Guide to the Universe

JOYA POPE

SAGE PUBLICATIONS
SAN MATEO

Sage Publications
Box 6944
San Mateo, CA 94403

For those Old Souls who've had interesting times
integrating themselves with this culture.

And for Maya.

Acknowledgments

This book would never have been written:

.....without the love, and perhaps the prodding, of my essence twin, Carl Ebnother—a Warrior—who kept insisting I "do" something.

.....without Marilyn Gordon's loving support throughout the entire process. She's willingly proof read every version and taught me rules about English. I can hardly wait to see her book!

.....without Steven Jobs and that elegant computer of his, the lovely Macintosh, which I've never struggled with; in fact, I haven't yet read the manual. Michael tells me I've written many lifetimes; unless I used to be word-perfect first draft, I don't see how I'd have ever had the patience without a computer.

.....without Chelsea Quinn Yarbro's "Messages from Michael" which attracted so many of us to the Michael System.

.....and finally, without JP Van Hulle and Aaron Christeaan who's delight in being themselves, as well as their spectacular ability to channel Michael, breathed life and fun into the teachings.

CONTENTS

CHAPTER ONE
DIFFERENT REALITIES

When I visit my mom, there inevitably comes a moment when she braces herself to ask, cheerily, "What have you been doing with yourself recently, dear?"

I too brace myself, for the truth. One of her steady warnings to me in childhood was, "Don't ever stray from the straight and narrow, and your life will work smoothly." Somehow, it was one of those lessons that never took, even back when I thought it important to try. And, as she knows, my life has been a bit bumpy.

"Channeling a being called Michael," I reply, as innocuously as possible.

I figured she'd ask what "channeling" was. Instead, she asks, hopefully this time, "Who's Michael?"

"Well, it is not simple to explain, Mom." I know a non-physical teacher is a fairly difficult notion to accept. It is also not a different lover from the one she has been shunning for the last few years. "Michael is actually just over one thousand people, well ex-people to be exact, sort of a multi-dimensional being. He, or they, live on another plane of existence and teach from there." She's agnostic, so I don't have to worry about taking away heaven and hell,

5

but I'm not at all sure she'll like hearing about astral or causal planes instead.

"You mean they are like the ghosts of a bunch of school teachers? This is starting to sound like the *National Enquirer* ."

Now she is getting alarmed. That is not a publication she finds amusing. "No, Mom, they teach about life because they are now in a more spiritually advanced place than we in our earthly set of lives. They are much clearer than 'ghosts' which sometimes hang around in buildings." I am dealing with a woman who has a Ph.D. in bio-chemistry and was once sure science would save the world. She might still be sure.

"You mean you can't see them at all?" She likes observable facts.

"Right. What I really meant was that the consciousness of Michael is clearer than your 'average ghost' who is still very much attracted to and usually upset by the earth plane. Also, because Michael has the information of over one thousand beings now at a very high level, he has a lot to say.

"Michael is not eerie at all, Mom. Rather, he is loving and caring as an evolved spiritual teacher would be, but not a sap either, if you know what I mean." From her look, she may not know. Mumbo jumbo.

"What is this 'channeling' business then?"

"It is the way people make contact with Michael." I decide not to tell her that the first Michael group used the Ouija board. I am positive I'd run into strong opinions about that.

So, I say, "What I do is set aside my personality and thoughts, get relaxed and balanced, and invite Michael in. Michael then actually uses my body and speaks in response to questions posed to him." She is looking at me like this might be a funny way of having sex. I add, "Sometimes channeling is invigorating for me and sometimes mildly tiring. We tape sessions because often I don't remember much of what was said." I am not sure that information helped.

"Mom, you look confused and apprehensive. Stick with me for a minute, OK? I look well and happy, right? Like I'm thriving? So put your worry aside for a minute and listen." She shrugs, acquiescing only for the moment.

I continue, "There are a number of people doing this in the San Francisco area. In fact the first group of people to start channeling Michael began over ten years ago in one of the plusher East Bay communities. They received a profusion of interesting information through this channeling and have had two widely circulated books published—by regular New York publishers. That would be akin to your research getting accepted in *Lancet* and then being picked up by *Time* .

"Even with the publication and acceptance of these books, members of this group still guard their identities carefully. They are all stable professional types, not unlike yourself, who were afraid of losing their credibility and perhaps their secure jobs should their metaphysical interests be publically exposed."

Though quiet, Mom's looking carefully at me. I am off the straight and narrow again. She is thinking it is for good reason that they protect their identities.

I am wondering if I should have protected mine. I also think it might be easier talking to the nation on Phil Donahue than talking to Mom, but I plunge ahead. "Mom, you know my friends. Not exactly tame, not a stolid one in the bunch, but no space-cadets either. Well, it's the same vibrant types who are now channeling Michael for private clients who have curiosity about why their lives have taken a certain shape. We also have a great magazine going, and several of us are working on books. The information we receive is just fascinating, very freeing. We can hardly wait to share it with a larger audience." Here comes that Phil Donahue fantasy again.

It looks like she has dropped the thought that perhaps

I am being duped into weird sex with some self-proclaimed off-the-planet being. Still, her expression is dubious, skeptical and worried. "Mom, let's shelve this and go for a walk on the beach. We'll talk about your career. I bet there is still lots of excitement there for you, right? Tonight you can read the introduction to my book and see if that makes more sense. I warn you though, it may expand your current definition of 'reality'."

Whew.

CHAPTER TWO
WHO'S MICHAEL?

For many, the Michael Teaching will fulfill a long-held, sometimes long-thwarted, desire to understand the vital principles behind life as experienced on our planet.

Though physics now has an incredibly interesting growing body of information about how this universe works, it doesn't seem to have the inmost heart of the information many are seeking. Therapy increases understanding of who's responsible for your life, as does the spectrum of available weekend groups, but what if your life is still more intense or difficult than most? "Why me?" is not an infrequent question. What if you grow so that you manage to maintain a positive attitude, keep your actions and communications responsible, enjoy loving relationships, but find yourself now judging others who haven't pulled themselves along as well? Judgments like that don't feel good, but how do you let the "laggards" off the hook? And how about the warmongers? You've learned the laws of manifesting, seen them work to a degree, and wonder what's holding back the rest of your dreams. Like physicists discovering the invisible patterns behind phenomena in our physical universe, reading Michael is to discover the invisibly large patterns behind our growth, evolution and day-to-day existences. Comprehend the pattern and life becomes more comfortable.

Most spiritual groups will tell you the bottom line is love; the corollary is to use love and trust to work positive changes in your life. And don't judge others. The problem, for many of the intellectual types in the Western World, is loving what looks reprehensible. Then, there is that age-old problem of being loving without being a doormat.

Michael is no different from other spiritual teachings in that the essential, underlying principle of the teaching is love—or as he often calls it, *agape*. Agape, a word taken from early Greek implying the unselfish love of a person for another without sexual implications, is used often because our English word "love" is forced to cover so much territory. Just as we don't have the words Eskimos or Arabs have to describe snow or sand, we don't have a variety to cover the many kinds of love. Try these for examples: "He's gorgeous and rich; I think I'm in love." or "I love Belgian chocolate the best of all." And how about this, "I loved her so much I nearly killed her when she saw another man."

While the primary purpose of the Michael teaching is agape or love, it is also an immensely practical philosophy designed to help make lives work better. Michael aids in understanding the deeper patterns of life, from the parts of life that seem unjust to those that feel veiled and mysterious. It is a teaching which so enhances the understanding of the differences between people that the mind relaxes, allowing the heart to then naturally open.

Many people dip into the Michael Teaching, get the information or insights they need, and then move on to the other groups or teachings which draw them. Some love the channeled information but miss a devotional type of experience, formal spirituality and ritual. And then there are those who easily skip all that and are happy as clams asking Michael nearly endless questions. Digging up new information becomes a fascination, which is not entirely intellectual, because growth and clarity seem to accelerate while lives feel more centered.

This is not an esoteric teaching designed to be kept hidden from the masses until they can wade through it in Martian or pay large fees to receive it. And, to the immense relief of many, Michael speaks with humor, in plain, easily understood English.

Michael's encyclopedic knowledge is continually emerging by means of a growing number of people accross the country who "channel" it while in light trance states. What we are receiving is a comprehensive description of life here on earth, which includes both large overviews about how life is organized, and as much personal detail as the inquiring person cares to uncover.

The channeling is now usually done verbally, not with the more cumbersome Ouija board. Channels must continually set aside their personalities and private beliefs to provide a clear passage for information. While most everyone has intuitive flashes, which are usually pieces of information getting through from other levels, channels learn to do it more consciously, in this case by drawing Michael in as a strong, felt, presence.

"Michael" is composed of 1050 individual essences, ex-humans so to speak, who have lived on the land part of earth, "graduated", and now teach, as part of their own progression, from another plane of existence. The group or entity is called "Michael" because the last person of the entity to finish lessons here and cycle-off the earth plane was named Michael in that final lifetime. When he was complete on earth, he merged with his awaiting entity and the whole then became known as Michael.

Similarly we are each composed of one individual essence, and are also part of an entity of 600 to 1200 individuals, many of whom we relate to and feel close with, lifetime to lifetime, while on earth. Each entity has a certain unique flavor. Some entities are very sweet by nature, others strong and solid; some are wildly expressive, others highly inspirational. The Michael entity looks at life in a careful, highly organized fashion and finds being practical and useful imperative.

Once the whole entity group is complete with the earth plane, it merges gradually into one being or consciousness, though the individual essences nevertheless retain some individuality. The goal and the deepest lessons, here or "there", are always agape, oneness, and unconditional love.

Later the entity, as part of its progression through the circle of existence, will also merge with other entities, first human, then cetacean (whales and dolphins), and finally entities of other sentient species from other planets in this universe. With every merging, the total information collected in every life by each individual, becomes available to all until eventually agape exists towards everything, the universe is understood and known. At this point, the merging with the Tao—or God— is complete.

If your credibility is strained, hold on to your hat; there's more to come!

But first, please realize one of the most basic and important principles of the Michael teaching is that of self-validation of all information received. Accept nothing on blind faith. Consult your own intuitive inner self as to the validity in your life of any information you find here. Weigh with your feelings. Channeling is not an exact science, though the accuracy level is usually very high, which is why people bother to learn to do it.

Michael's teaching is simply one way to look at the world; so if it doesn't fit for you, set it aside. Similarly, if a particular piece of information does not feel right, set it aside while keeping what does feel right, using what you find useful. Michael is a strong presence and can be quite forceful with what he's presenting, so it is important to always self-validate.

Even though we use Michael in this teaching as a resource and a teacher, we do not use him as an authority figure or a guru. Michael is neither a religion nor a belief system.

There are different schools and teachings that lead one to truth and growth. This teaching is the path of love. Michael tells us, "The school of obedience is the most appropriate for *Baby Souls* [see next chapter]. The school of 'hard knocks' is the most appropriate for *Young Souls*. The school of intellectual pursuit and non-identification is the most appropriate for *Mature Souls*. The school of love is always appropriate and the only school consistently attractive to *Old Souls*."

CHAPTER THREE
THE SOUL AGES

Michael affirms what we've suspected; life is indeed a learning game. He then goes on to describe the structure and rules of this game, patterns much too big to be perceived easily while living in their midst.

To begin the game, sparks of consciousness (entities) who are attracted to experience on the earth plane cast themselves out from the Tao (God—the birthplace of all souls) and divide into between 600 and 1200 individual fragments or essences. By portioning itself in this way, the ever-curious entity, which starts as one consciousness, can gather incredible amounts of experience and thus satisfy this curiosity in shorter periods of time. The individual essences in the entity gradually start incarnating, over many hundreds of years, onto the earth as individual humans.

Soul age refers to how a person has grown from experience on the planet, not just how many lifetimes he or she has lived.

Each physical plane existence changes and deepens the essence's point of view. The structure is to go through the developmental levels Michael calls **Infant, Baby, Young, Mature,** and **Old Soul** levels. Each will take a minimum of seven lifetimes, more likely around twenty.

After that there are six other planes of existence to grow through, and then it's back to the oneness of the Tao. This is an extraordinarily long "game" we are talking about, especially from our earthly perspective.

No person, essence or entity is "ahead" or "behind" any other, but is simply occupying another place in the continuous circle leading to and from the Tao. Ways of being are supposed to be different in different developmental stages; at some point we experience it all, moving continually along to different levels of understanding and responsibility. Michael always emphasizes that while each stage is unique and manifestly distinct from the others, no one place is better or worse than any other; they all belong in this game we have chosen to play.

INFANT SOULS

The fragment, or essence, just cast out from the Tao, is raw, without experience, and usually enmeshed in a struggle over physical survival on the unfamiliar earth plane. Thus the Infant Soul stage is one characterized by many fears. In this stage people are often born into primitive, sometimes tribal conditions. Learning how to survive is the primary concern, so Infant Souls learn to identify and find roots, berries and other edibles. They fish and hunt, grow food, build shelter, keep warm or cool, and stay away from predators.

To our eyes, these look like pretty rough lifetimes. They are often short. Starvation, isolation, drought, floods, hurricanes, earthquakes, tigers, bears, poisonous snakes and combat are experienced along with every other survival threat imaginable.

On the positive side, being so fresh from the Tao can give a mystical flavor to Infant Souls. They resonate closely with nature and many times feel not individuation

16

but great oneness with everyone in their family or tribe. They can be intuitive and earthy in a simple, unquestioning way. They have the knack, all too soon forgotten, for living in the moment.

The intellectual center does not become fully opened in this phase, and there isn't yet much feeling for ethics or personal morality. The Infant Soul has to be taught what is right and wrong. Even a highly intelligent person may seem dull or not quite pulled together with his or her thinking .

Cooking and eating are strictly exercises in survival, not even close to being opportunities for optimizing pleasure. Love or sexuality will be experienced on the level of lust. Questions like, "How can I get him (or her) to like me?" basically do not arise unless it becomes a survival issue. Survival is what is important, and whatever needs to be done for survival is done. The Infant Soul can sometimes be driven to violence or extreme self-protective behavior by a merely unfamilar happening.

Infant Souls tend to cluster around the equator because the constant climate makes some aspects of survival more simple. Rural Guatamala, El Salvador, Ethiopia, Sudan and the Amazon basin are areas with predominately Infant Souls; Iraq and Iran have them in increasing numbers.

The earth is close to the time when the last Infant Soul will incarnate. Many fewer are beginning incarnation here now than even one hundred years ago. Though there are still many entities checking us out, most will decide to go elsewhere. The planet is looking a little worn.

Our society is too perplexing and complex in its demands to be a place Infant Souls feel comfortable choosing. When found in the United States (which is rare), they will generally gravitate towards less populated, "backwoods" areas. Infant Souls will not tend to seek regular employment because it is too complicated and involving to handle. Usually living on the fringes of society, they are often viewed by the rest of the population as inept or slightly out of tune.

Infant Souls rarely come into prominence except through notoriety. Richard Ramirez, California's serial murderer who became known as the Nightstalker, exemplifies that type of fame. He is a late Infant Soul enmeshed in a lifetime of intense experience and intense karma formation.

BABY SOULS

There are seven discrete parts *within* each of the Soul ages, each taking somewhere between one to ten lifetimes for completion. Thus when a person is complete with all seven levels of Infant, the consciousness will start to explore the early Baby Soul process.

As a Baby Soul, since there is now a little experience on the earth, more sophistication and less fear are found, though the world is still seen as a scary place. Survival has been worked out; this is a time to get civilized and be proud of it, a time of demonstrating you can do it right.

Structure helps Baby Souls to feel comfortable in the world. They want to be directed and therefore seek out higher authorities who are willing to lay out clear rules. As a small example of this, they would rarely defend their child to the school principal, but push to make the child act acceptably to the teachers and administration. Sometimes a Baby Soul will seek out—even again and again—discipline from the prison system as a way to civilize himself. This soul age will hold traditional religious leaders in esteem, turn doctors into gods, while politicians they like can do no wrong.

Traditions, rituals, and law and order provide a welcome sense of security. "That's the rule and that's what we'll do," is typical thinking . They make sure your car is not parked in front of their house and that their lawn is mowed. In a dogmatic, black-and-white way, they know right from wrong. Usually conscientiously good citizens, they can be counted on to do the "right" thing. This is also the soul age with the greatest propensity to long-term grudge holding.

The Ku Klux Klan would be a Baby Soul organization in a negative pole, while many service organizations like the Knights of Columbus or the Rotary Club would be in a more positive pole of expression. Anti-abortion right-to-life organizations, school prayer promoters, and fire-and-brimstone preachers all tend to emerge out of Baby Soul consciousness and concerns.

Preferring to be big fish in small ponds, Baby Souls are often found in small communities. Though the United States is primarily a Young Soul country, middle America between the two coasts is packed with Baby Souls who prefer life when it is a little simpler. They often emerge as pillars of the community, staunch, upright and unshakable in their beliefs. They become mayor or sheriff, president of the town council or PTA. Because they are interested in organizing and developing the fabric of society with laws, regulations and lines of authority, they are often found in governmental bureaucracies such as schools, hospitals, regulating agencies and so on.

When their beliefs are opposed, Baby Souls may become inwardly bewildered. Baby Souls are so sure they are right that they have difficulty comprehending opposition. This is not a self-reflective phase.

Many patriotic Baby Soul soldiers coming back from Vietnam were perplexed and confounded. Their country had changed; there were no heros' welcomes. Usually a Baby Soul won't show inner quandary; when perplexed or thwarted there is more likely to be an outward display of belligerence. Baby Souls feel justified in fighting for their beliefs and may demonstrate not just dogmatism but a fairly brutal mentality.

They are very interested, if not obsessive, about cleanliness, neatness, and keeping germs at bay. Not yet able to perceive that chronic feelings or attitudes may cause physical and psychological problems, their emotional difficulties are, in fact, often somaticized so that angry feelings become gallstones, or fear turns into kidney, bladder or back trouble.

When dealing with physical problems like these, Baby Souls usually prefer conventional medicine, medications and surgery. Considering alternative therapies or looking for the root of the problem doesn't make sense to their way of approaching the body. With the exception of the new popularity of healing within charismatic churches, this soul age is sold on orthodox medicine.

Around sexual matters, there is uneasiness and some degree of shame or guilt. This is not a time for hot-tub entertaining, but hiding bodies, making love in the dark—probably with pajamas and without great sensuality.

Families, however, feel very good during this period. Raising children (maybe lots), seeing relatives, celebrating holidays, going on family outings and participating in church rituals all make a person feel a solid upstanding part of the community.

Many of the people who create what we call folk art or naive art are Baby Souls expressing their values and concerns. You see pictures of the countryside, church picnics, Bible stories, family weddings, the 4th of July and ships with proud flags waving in the breeze. The paintings can be quite lovely, though neither perspective nor method of presentation is sophisticated.

Baby Souls sometimes come into prominence. They don't often look for a big stage, not having the resourcefulness or experience to handle it well, but they may gather fame for their unyielding political or religious beliefs. Jerry Falwell is a prominent religious leader with Baby Soul beliefs. Idi Amin, Hitler, Khomeini, and, in the United States, President Nixon and some of our more conservative Governors, Congressmen and Senators are examples of Baby Souls putting out their world views on a larger scale.

President Botha of South Africa and Colonel Khadafy of Libya are both seventh level Baby Souls. The seventh level of any Soul age is a time of complacency and smugness, because everything at that Soul level *has* been handled. (The next lifetime, of course, finds a person uneasily in the first level of a totally new consciousness phase.)

Baby Soul countries often have a puritanical tinge and may be divided against themselves or a close neighbor. Countries expressing a primarily Baby Soul perceptivity are Iran and Iraq and most of the newly strict Muslim countries, though not Saudi Arabia or Syria; also included are Ireland, Costa Rica, and much of South America. India, which historically was an Old Soul country, is now mostly late Baby, poised to enter the Young Soul phase. Interestingly, the whites who rule South Africa are mainly Baby Souls while the blacks are primarily Mature Souls.

YOUNG SOULS

Having mastered Infant and Baby Soul issues of survival, discipline and order, the essence is now looking to see how powerful it can become in the world.

Independence and the ability to get what one wants out of life are the driving force of the Young Soul stage. Seizing what the physical plane has to offer, vying to gain positions of prominence, power and great wealth, causes this to become the most competitive period in the whole cycle of lifetimes. Those who are expressing themselves from Young Soul perceptivity will tend towards a sort of tape measure mentality that makes them monitor who among them has the fattest bank account, the best parties or invitations, the greatest weekly aerobic output, the tallest building, fastest motorcycle, broadest shoulders, thinnest hips or biggest diamonds..

21

The most powerful places in the world—Japan, Hong Kong, Germany, Israel, Syria, Saudi Arabia, Canada and the United States—all express a strong Young Soul perceptivity. All people growing up in these places, regardless of their soul ages, will receive Young Soul "imprinting" or conditioning about how they should run their lives to be a success.

Ambition is important with the attitude being, "There is you and there is me, and I am going to win." There is a great drive to get ahead. In the process of getting to the top, it doesn't matter too much what needs to be done or who's stepped on and over.

If one can make money or gain influence, the long term consequences of any act aren't terribly important. The problem with toxic wastes being dumped all over is one result of being in a Young Soul culture in a hurry to make a buck. While Young Souls are productive, industrious and goal oriented, their vision extends only so far, and they don't often question their motives.

Because they are desirous of making something of themselves and leaving their mark on the world, Young Souls can be tireless workers. We owe them our efficiency, much of our high technology, our military might, and our continual push to make things happen and change. They are the architects of civilization and its builders. However, with the focus on quantity and not necessarily on quality, something like scientific agriculture will be valued and the fact that it poisons the earth with pesticides and ecological problems would be little noticed. Bumper crops are bumper crops.

Young Souls don't always pursue what they like, which they may see as an indulgence, but what they believe will create success. They learn how the system works early on and use it to their advantage. Driven towards achievement, they flock to large well-known universities so they can get degrees of prominence. Some of these people seem born with the ability to make the economic system jump through hoops of their own design, turning their hundreds into thousands and their millions into billions with apparent ease.

The essence of a man (or woman) at the Young Soul stage will actually be pushing him to acquire as much as he can in order to soak in how it feels. He will covet prestigious cars and itch to live in a "better" area inside the most impressive house he can afford. Great silent estates somewhat smaller than Buckingham Palace with twelve foot walls, ornamental hedges or fountains, radio-operated wrought-iron gates, and serious art collections may be obtainable during some lifetimes in the Young Soul phase. If your Young Soul glory days were spent in ancient Egypt, your riches took a slightly different form and no doubt included slaves and plenty of wealth for the afterlife.

Not much laziness in this period, though you can find Young Souls shoving things in closets or drawers just before people come over. That has to do with priorities being more out in the world, not laziness. Baby Souls tend toward compulsive neatness, while the Young period is concerned with success and appearances.

Because Young Souls are not emotionally open, they tend to make poor parents who don't make strong feeling connections with their children. However they will buy their children everything they can afford. Like the prototype Yuppie baby in an Aprica stroller and French clothing, children become status objects for their parents. These children with expensive haircuts, cars and educations, will be pushed to excel in all they do from nursery school, through college, to marriage and career. Those successes will reflect favorably back on the status-seeking parent.

Young Souls tend to be conventional but less adamant than Baby Souls in their religious beliefs. You'll likely find them networking at church, promoting their businesses.

Because Young Souls are heavily identified with their bodies and really not sure that consciousness survives it, we have plastic surgery for noses and elbows, thighs and chins, breasts and waists; a booming multi-billion dollar industry devoted to beauty products for men *and* women and an incredibly huge and costly (Young Soul, high-tech) medical system which intends on keeping everyone alive as long as possible regardless of desires, costs, pain, or quality of life.

Towards the end of the Young cycle, people will start to experiment more with food and sex. They'll likely become adventurous with extensive travel, both to experience the world, their oyster, and to gain status among peers.

As superb manipulators of the environment, humans are unequivocally good at the Young Soul phase. Winning out over rivals, accomplishment, power and money make them feel on top of the world.

Admittedly there is incredible stress, but overall, this is an essentially exciting, fulfilling time. Because the earth is still in its Young Soul phase, acknowledgement for Young Souls, who are already outgoing go-getters, comes along quite easily.

Creativity opens up during this phase, although it comes to a fuller fruition in the Mature phase. Many, many, people rise to fame and prominence during this period; we find movie stars, TV newscasters, singers, comics, politicians, religious leaders, Nobel prize winners, Hollywood producers, authors, and people, like Jean-Paul Getty, who get so rich they get famous.

Two famously avaricious couples exemplify in extreme what can be the Young Soul grasp for wealth and power at any price. They are Ferdinand and Imelda Marcos, formerly of the Philippines, and Jean-Claude and Michele Duvalier, formerly of Haiti. Neither pair seems to experience regret for their actions nor have suspicion of the extensive karma created.

Like Ronald Reagan, many of our Presidents are Mature Souls. John Kennedy, a Young Soul, nearly had to be that in order to have the ambition and energy required to break down significant barriers against Catholics. Similarly, Geraldine Ferraro used her energy and drive as a Young Soul to loosen the obstructions against women entering the White House. Gorbachev is a late Young Soul beginning to check out Mature Soul behaviors. Being mid-Young helps Margaret Thatcher have the spine and ambition to hold her position. Professors at our most prestigious universities are often Young Souls, as are most of the people in responsible positions at major corporations.

Johnny Carson, Jack Benny and Bob Hope are wonderful examples of Young Soul show business personalities, while Dick Cavett, Lennie Bruce and Bette Midler would be examples of show biz types with a Mature Soul flavor. Rose Kennedy, the driving force behind the Kennedy clan for decades, is a Young Soul with a will of iron. Mohammed Ali, who viewed life as a contest, is a grand Young Soul sports personality. Mick Jagger is the quintessential Young Soul rock personality, and Billy Graham, a quite powerful Young Soul religious leader.

MATURE SOULS

By the end of the Young Soul phase, an uneasiness arises that something is amiss. All the wealth, power and acclaim aren't quite enough; gain no longer has transcendental value. Thus begins the search of the Mature Soul period. The questions "Who am I? Why am I here?" are asked with frequency in these lives. These are trying, intense times; emotions open up, boundaries between people break down. Seeing another person's point of view becomes possible as people become deeply immersed in relationship issues. Suddenly it's clear everybody has feelings, and these feelings are interesting, if not unavoidable.

One of the reasons Young Souls are able to direct so

much energy towards success is that their inner lives aren't calling for attention, so their energy flows easily towards externals. Not so in the Mature period. It is a very introspective time. There is more emotional centering here, more intensity, more schizophrenia, more pain, more suicide, more love, more sensuality, and probably more drugs to intensify it all than in any other period.

Creativity flows. Philosophy and art come into prominence. Illusion and distortion of reality are inevitable as a person opens up because there is not a clear path nor an easy way to sort through all the feelings. Nothing is so solid as in the Baby and Young phases.

Being flexible is not easy. Until the last couple of decades our culture provided few guideposts for this vexing set of lives. The hippies with all their "flow" and "beingness" facilitated everyone's understanding of the Mature Soul phase and helped disassemble some of this society's blinder adulation of Young Soul consciousness.

Because they are often misunderstood and perceived as disturbed, when actually just perceiving more than the Young Soul, Mature Souls will often gravitate towards a community of other Mature Souls where they can be understood. Berkeley and Cambridge are two notoriously Mature Soul cities in the United States, as is Amsterdam in Holland. The gay men's communities in Hollywood and San Francisco are a mixture, but tend to be Mature in flavor.

Mature Souls will enjoy the company of other Mature Souls for the "being on the same path" feeling, as well as for the intensity. They will enjoy Old Souls for information and an occasional rest and Young Souls for their reminders of how to push forward in the world.

This, like the Young Soul phase, is a time when many rise to prominence, though less now through ambition and power, and more from vim, verve and dash. Notice the individual's character tends to be full, usually quite interesting and creative. Painter Vincent Van Gogh suffered continually from the intensity of his feelings, while Paul

Gauguin hoped to find solace from them in a peaceful Tahiti. We have actors Marilyn Monroe, Marlon Brando, Elizabeth Taylor, Richard Burton, Lily Tomlin, Jane Fonda and Donald Sutherland; there are pop stars Michael Jackson, Paul McCartney, Madonna and Boy George; whiz kid Steven Jobs; crusaders Ralph Nader and Tom Hayden; and spiritual searchers and authors Carlos Castaneda and Lynn Andrews. And, let's not forget, Barbara Walters, the TV interviewer who is *always* interested in what people feel. Abigail van Buren of "Dear Abby" fame is a Mature Soul, while her twin sister, Ann Landers, an advice columnist with stricter views, is a late Baby Soul.

Mature Souls will seek higher education but gravitate towards smaller non-traditional schools. This period has its own priorities and inner sense of direction. For example, Mature Souls will sometimes, much to the bewilderment of their Young Soul relatives, purposefully turn away from a well-paying, high status position to choose something more in line with their developing priorities, whether more casual, more risky and creative, or more save-the-world.

This whole period is marked by exploration, much of it inner. Non-traditional religions, meditation, and metaphysics start to look interesting, while outer horizons broaden with unfastened lifestyles, sex of all sorts, art of all types, gourmet and foreign food.

Countries with Mature Soul attributes will tend to have more attention on social relationships than on material goods or efficiency. Examples are Italy, Greece, Egypt, and Mexico. England is a little off balance due to its recent entry into the Mature phase. With the advent of a socialism which aims for an equal distribution of wealth, you also have the average Briton, now also in the Mature phase, suddenly more interested in his or her inner life than in a hard struggle to maintain a power position in the world. People are less interested in nose-to-the-grindstone hard work, but it is not because their very basic survival is handled by the socialistic system. It is because they have changed on an inner level.

Poland and Russia are countries brimming with Mature Souls where strong agreements exist for assets to be divided fairly, for everyone to have equal shares of the wealth. Marxist theory is very much Mature Soul in flavor, if not in actuality. The ruling groups in both those countries are heavy, hardy Young Soul types who have managed, through thick and thin, by hook and crook, to hang on to the power.

OLD SOULS

On deep inner levels, Old Souls perceive the interrelatedness existing among all people. Intuitively they sense they are part of an integral whole. Grasping this big picture, Old Souls then do their best to live by it and to not harm or judge others. There is a strong urge to be impeccable and to maintain personal integrity in all transactions.

Having numerous lifetimes in a variety of cultures and classes thoroughly blended into their essence, it is much more difficult for Old Souls to get embroiled in the right-and-wrong, us-and-them games people and countries both play. Seeing the whole picture can make Old Souls appear almost passive to the other soul ages.

While Old Souls do not tend to grow into their full soul perceptivity until about age thirty-five or so, they will, even before then, be accused of stepping to the beat of a different drummer. They are unusual—two steps away from the norm—in a Young Soul culture. Since they individualistically follow their inner perceptions and desires, they may be seen as eccentric, though usually harmlessly so.

While there is great motivation for spiritual growth, motivation tends to be lacking when it comes to developing political or material punch. Seldom doing anything they don't want to and preferring their own unconventional pursuits, they often seek the path of least resistance as far as work, so that all energy can be poured into spiritual development.

Because of the essence's richness gathered over many lifetimes, Old Souls tend to be extremely competent in a wide range of things—which often aren't pursued. They will try to find work that supports their personal growth: counseling, teaching, gardening, carpentry and bodywork being some favorites. Many are magnetized by philosophy and art. If higher education proves necessary in order to teach, less orthodox schools allowing more opportunities for inner exploration will be favored.

A fancy house or car, or impressive clothes and jewels aren't often high on an Old Soul's real priority list. Neither is a nine-to-five job. Laziness on the physical plane sometimes creates difficulties paying the bills, but the material game just isn't what it used to be. However, Old Souls do have one advantage with the material plane. As they begin to seek, understand and use the laws of the physical universe, goals can be attained with less effort.

Old Souls may explore many religions and teachings, being most drawn to those emphasizing love and to those they've resonated with closely in past lives. But being as disciplined or orthodox as some practices require does not usually last long. Unique, personal spiritual practices, like an oceanside ritual for a birthday, are often developed and used by Old Souls.

Old Souls are very capable of agape or unconditional love, and many consciously work on not *ever* judging other people. On the other hand, some Old Souls appear to be annoyingly remote. This is usually an essence who has previously handled all emotional issues and comes to the planet planning on learning intellectual, philosophical and spiritual issues, period. In Shirley MacLaine's television miniseries, *Out on a Limb,* the character, David, who took her to Peru and never stopped playing teacher, was quite

29

lacking in warmth. David's personality appeared to function well with minimal feeling; he didn't seem to mind being that way at all. But some personalities go crazy with the dry lack of emotional connectedness and go about "fixing" the apparent lack, but the force of essence—which is committed only to getting spiritual lessons—will not be behind creating the change. This does not mean the change can't be made; just that it is trickier to pull off.

A similar situation arises after a person has had materially successful lifetimes. The essence has completed the lessons to be gained from having riches and does not have much impetus to recreate those situations except as it might peripherally help with other lessons. Your essence may be willing to let you be dirt poor for the duration of your lifetimes as long as it is gaining the desired spiritual and philosophic lessons.

Remember, you are your essence while you are astral; it is you who decides not to give yourself the wealthy Young Soul parents or the drive and ambition to go out and get powerfully rich. The problem is, of course, that when you arrive on the physical plane, the personality goes a little crazy without material goodies in a material world. The personality may push to make a comfortable living, and pull it off, but again without the added impetus of essence saying, "Make a bundle." and "You have got to be successful." As long as the essence is being fed what it really wants—philosophical and spiritual food—it won't hamper your goals of making money or creating warm, emotional connectedness with people. But essence still won't be propelling you toward prosperity or emotionally nourishing relationships.

A major challenge of the Old Soul period is mastering self-esteem. No one is complete until there is forgiveness and self-love. Self-esteem can be elusive when living in a Young Soul society which doesn't acknowledge the work or innate value of most older souls. And on top of that, Old Souls truly see what a small part they play in an infinite universe. They, therefore, often make a very big deal out of working this one through, using lots of self-deprecation along the way.

While Old Soul's are often the sex they least prefer, having had male and female bodies so many times in past lives, they begin to blend them more and are not greatly identified with being either male or female. It's hard to work up a lather about someone's homosexuality or "lack of masculinity" or "femininity". Bisexual feelings are not uncommon; whether acted upon or not, they are allowed to rise to the surface, sometimes. Sex which takes on a cosmic feeling becomes possible and sought after.

Seeing a very Old Soul as a baby is telling, for while the child is still acting the demanding infant or growing baby, another quality may be sensed. Because the soul has done all of this so many times, the child has a peace, ease, and wisdom about it—at least in its quieter moments—that is sensed by the adults around it.

Many fewer Old Souls than Mature or Young ones become famous, and when they do it is to teach, for the Old Soul level is the teaching level. None of us complete the physical plane experience until everything we've learned is shared with at least one other person.

People typifying this Old Soul need to teach are John Lennon and Yoko Ono, Bob Marley, film director John Boorman (*Emerald Forest, Deliverance*), author Alice Walker (*The Color Purple*), Shirley MacLaine, Phil Donahue, Mark Twain, John Muir, and Albert Einstein. Directly on the spiritual front, we find Don Juan Matus, Nostradamus, Gurdjieff, Carl Jung, Werner Erhard, Rajneesh, Ram Dass, and Swamis Satchidananda, Muktananda and Chidvilasananda. Anatoly Shcharansky, Abraham Lincoln, Anwar Sadat and Saudi Arabia's former Oil Minister Saki Yamani are four Old Souls who put their energy into the political arena. You'll notice each of these people teaches from their being, in a unique, very individual fashion, which isn't at all what society usually recognizes as

31

teaching.

Countries currently containing predominately Old Souls (but not necessarily Old Soul leadership) are Iceland, Holland, Switzerland and Czechoslovakia. Old Soul nations prefer neutrality in international conflicts, and when that's impossible, they prefer subjugation to violence and bloodshed. Being aware that freedom is first an inner experience, they teach their captors a great deal about harmony and humanity. Historically we see this in Alexander the Great's conquest of (then Old Soul) Persia and parts of what is now modern India.

Old Souls are everywhere, sprinkled fairly thinly. The United States has pockets of Old Souls, primarily in California—with the greatest number residing in the northern end of the state—and in Florida, especially the Keys. Certain other cities, like Santa Fe and Taos, both in New Mexico, take on a comfortable Old Soul flavor. Russia also has large scale Old Soul pockets, the major one now unfortunately being in Siberia. Michael said that all these Old Souls incarnated in the U.S.S.R. to help push that country forward. They did not expect to end up in Gulags, nor would they have chosen that way to work. Even the best laid astral plans don't always pan out perfectly.

Many individual Old Souls are scattered about, resting in comfortable island places like Tahiti, or conversely, working spiritedly in places like Africa to help bring a country or continent forward. Old Souls incarnate in Infant Soul areas like the Amazon in order to protect, aid, assist, foster, nourish and guide those that need it.

PRACTICALITIES

There is a tendency for older souls to have a greater understanding of what the younger soul perceptivities are like than vice-versa. Knowing about perceptivity is exceedingly helpful in understanding both the way other individuals look at life and something about their life task.

Each soul age is trying to experience as much as possible within that particular level of perceptivity. It's absolutely appropriate for an Infant Soul to be fearfully concerned about basic survival and for a Baby Soul to be requesting law and order. A Young Soul is appropriate when striving for great material wealth, power and acclaim, while a Mature Soul when beginning to ask deep questions and feel intensely emotional. It's appropriate for an Old Soul to not meet societal norms, to look and act mildly eccentric and to be teaching others, even when his own personal or material life isn't together.

To expect your Old Soul child to make a successful climb up some corporate ladder is unrealistic. Likewise, it's in error to expect an aggressive Young Soul attorney to turn her attention towards saving the environment; or to imagine a Mature Soul embroiled in some emotional drama would be able to calm down because you show him the "big picture".

An Old Soul starts each lifetime being born as an infant who experiences Infant Soul consciousness and gradually grows into prior levels of consciousness. A baby is often perceiving through Baby Soul consciousness; think about a two year old shrieking because a parent offended her sense of right and wrong. People vary, but generally reach the competitive Young Soul consciousness sometime in the grade school years. And Mature Soul consciousness is what your up-and-down, full-of-drama, teenager is experiencing.

Individuals don't come close to obtaining their true soul perceptivity roughly one-third of the time. They get stuck. They get lazy. Or the essence finds it easier to complete certain karmas at earlier more ambitious or more emotional soul levels.

While most Old Souls (Mature Souls too) will be doing the intense Mature phase in their teens and early twenties, an Old Soul is often not consistently acting out of Old Soul awareness until about age thirty-five, and even then it may be only in some areas of life and not others. When security buttons get pushed for instance, it is often difficult to remain completely in Old Soul consciousness.

Old Souls will be able to drop out some of the Baby Soul discipline, Young Soul ambition, and Mature Soul emotionality successfully *only if* those qualities are integrated sufficiently into their personality that they have access to them when necessary. It does not work to stick nose-in-air (or head-in-sand) in an attempt to avoid lessons and gifts from the other soul ages.

People who come into the Michael teaching are usually relieved to find out why they are different from mainstream society. They always knew it anyway. It's helpful to get the explanation and understand why it is that some share their global perspectives and others, no matter how intelligent, just aren't interested. Because many Old Souls have experienced being made wrong by younger souls, there is some tendency towards backlash. This may take the form of an assumed spiritual superiority. Some people may lecture or start to look down their noses at the "younger" masses.

The purpose of the teaching is agape, not creating yourself to be one up. Younger souls are not less intelligent, less appropriate or wrong. Their lessons are about survival, structure, ambition and success, while your lessons are about emotional and universal connections. Younger souls are a natural part of that whole you <u>know</u> is all connected, right? So, if you're indulging yourself in this way, aim for mild tolerance as a way to begin clearing up this attitude, which ultimately is a painful, burdensome one to carry around.

THE SEVEN LEVELS
WITHIN EACH SOUL AGE

Each of these soul ages has seven distinct stages, so

an individual can be referred to as a fourth level Old Soul or a seventh level Old Soul. A level gives a distinct flavor to the lifetimes spent within its arena. Except for the sixth, each level takes about three lifetimes to complete, though some essences speed through faster, while the solid types enjoy a more thorough, leisurely pace.

A description of each level is given below along with examples of people in that level. You can see how each level effects a lifetime's behavior. The reason there are so many more people listed in some of the levels is because those are the places that lend themselves more easily to comfort with a fair amount of public attention.

The *first level* is a tentative exploration of the new soul age, kind of a feeler or probe. There is a sense of uneasiness, and people at this level will usually spend about 70% of their time back in the comfortably familiar level just completed. The first level is enough of a trial balloon that it does not give itself to center stage behaviors.

The *second level,* though cozier, still has much push and pull. People begin to realize they can function best by forging ahead into the new consciousness and that the former perceptivity keeps them frustrated; yet they aren't sure of their footing within the new level at all. Alice Walker, who wrote *The Color Purple,* is second level Old as is Actor Dustin Hoffman. Prince Charles is second level Mature but held back by much Baby Soul imprinting which his wife is pushing to eliminate so that their lives can be more fun. Ronald Reagan is another example of second Mature, but with a wife who prefers to keep him at her soul age, Young.

The *third level* begins to gain the full perceptivity of the new soul age internally, but has difficulty manifesting it in the world. The person becomes extremely introverted and intellectually introspective while trying to integrate the new awarenesses into day-to-day life. Public television's financial show host, Louis Rukeyser, is at third level Mature. With his *Wall Street Week* television show he is

35

more "out there" than most at this level. Both his goal of growth and chief feature of arrogance [see chapter on "Overleaves"] give him a push that is clearly somewhat uncomfortable to his essentially introspective nature. Ralph Nader is another third level Mature person who allows his goals and principles to push him into the limelight despite his desire for quiet introversion.

Fourth level, bingo. Integrated and consolidated, the perceptivity is now both inner and outer. Comfortable and feeling assured while pushing out into the world, fourth level lifetimes are spent in full swing, doing and achieving any number of things—perhaps forming a bit of karma along the way. Singer/Poet Bob Dylan moves between third and fourth levels. Pope John Paul II, Fidel Castro, and Terry Cole-Whittaker are all fourth level Mature, while Imelda and Ferdinand Marcos, California's Ed Zschau and Syria's President Assad are fourth Young. Phil Donahue and Rama (a California spiritual teacher) are both busy, fourth level Old Souls.

Fifth level people start pushing on the limits of their reassuring fourth level existences. Believe it or not, humans don't stick with comfort long, especially when it starts impinging on growth. Leaving the beaten path for exploration, experimentation and the unorthodox, this level stretches every point and often shows up as pretty eccentric in the process. The person may feel disquieted, out of his element, and would often be taken to be a younger soul age than his fourth level friends. Madonna goes from a solid, businesslike fourth level to a very unconventional fifth and back again with fair regularity; PeeWee Herman is quite fifth level Mature most all the time as was the enigmatic Andy Warhol. Bette Midler is yet another fifth level Mature person who appears to be writing her own book on unique behavior. Zsuzanna Budapest, the feminist witch who leads the Susan B. Anthony coven, and Gary Larson, the sweet, very shy creator of the extremely bizarre *The Far Side* cartoons, are both Old Souls manifesting at fifth level. Sage

Ken Kesey of *The Electric Kool-Aid Acid Test* fame is a Mature fifth level eccentric starting to dip into the karmic sixth level.

Sixth level pieces together the experiences of the prior levels and starts handling obligations incurred along the way. This means accumulated karmic debts get paid back through numerous, intense, nearly overfilled sixth level lives. A person will likely have trouble after hard luck and be at wits end from all the calamitous action coming her way. These sixth level catch-up lives are a difficult and demanding group, usually taking longer to complete than any other level. As an Old Soul, these lives are truly the last chance for *all* karmic completions, some of which have been avoided for dozens upon dozens of lifetimes.

Think about what's been jammed into these sixth level lives: John Kennedy, Elizabeth Taylor, Jesse Jackson, Timothy Leary, Rajneesh, Jeremy Rifkin, Deng Xiaoping and Stephen Jobs. Joe Kennedy II, who now holds an elective office, is a Mature sixth level Sage likely to have a lot of news-making incidents occurring in his life. Richard Ramirez, at sixth level Infant, is creating as well as handling large amounts of karma. Old Souls Ram Dass and Yogi Bhajan appear to have completed the last of their sixth level intensities in this lifetime and have moved on to a smoother seventh level consciousness

Whew, *seventh level!* The karma's paid; it's time for some well earned poise, rest and complacency. Not too many obstructions or impeding subplots here; seventh level lives usually unfold somewhat gracefully. Having freshly understood the lessons themselves, individuals are in a good position to teach others—especially those of the soul age just completed. For Old Souls, there is an urgency to share their perceptivity and ways of being with others.

Moamar Khadafy and P.W. Botha, both at seventh level Baby, don't have lives that flow as well as some, but are tenacious enough with their beliefs, even under fire, to display that seventh level complacency which can be maddening when you happen to disagree. Mature and Old seventh level lives definitely flow. Actors Alec Guinnes and Danny deVito, author Frank Herbert, sexologist Ruth Westheimer, Speaker of the House Tip O'Neill and comedian Robin Williams are all seventh Mature. Spiritual teachers Swami Muktananda and Swami Satchidananda are seventh level Old.

CHAPTER FOUR
THE ROLES

Essence leaving the Tao is like pure white light travelling through a prism, refracting into one of seven colors, or in this case, *roles*. These roles introduce variety into life experience, like a rainbow of colors to white light. The essence, once it has adopted a role, keeps it for each lifetime of the cycle (from Infant through Old and on), developing that role—feeling, tasting and understanding everything in life from that role's particular perspective. Each role serves a function for the other roles; for example, one role is for fun and lightness, another for structure and rule enforcement, and yet another for creating what's needed—often by breaking all the rules. Together, all the roles weave the patterns of human interaction we observe on this planet.

An individual's role is actually more comforting than confining. The flavor it gives to a person is about the *only* thing which remains constant from life to life. Learning about the role tells people, in a very rich manner, what they are about on a very basic level; it tells them what doesn't change and what part they play when interacting with others and life. In that way, it cuts deeper than either astrology or what Michael calls the personality's overleaves, because all of that does change life to life. And thank goodness it does, or we'd all be bored to tears.

Having knowledge of one's role usually increases self-acceptance. As people resonate with the sense of their role and are more freely able to express themselves in a way that is natural to them in the first place, life becomes easier.

There are seven roles in all, three of them paired. Artisan and Sage are the *expressive* roles, the people most gifted at communicating ideas and feelings; Server and Priest are the *inspirational* pair, giving and compassionate; while Warrior and King are the *action* roles characterized by groundedness, physicality, and productivity. Scholar is the neutral or *assimilative* role which excels at organizing and absorbing information. All these role names refer to ways of perceiving the world, which are discussed below, and not to any kind of career definitions.

Each of the pairs resonate with each other, often easily enjoying its sister role because of many similarities. The first of each pair—Artisan, Server and Warrior—is called an *ordinal* role while the second part of the pair—Sage, Priest and King, is called *exalted*. Scholars have the ability to act from either point of view.

Ordinal roles, in most lifetimes, prefer intimate, one-to-one ties with people and may tend to be uncomfortable or withdraw from large groups while the exalted roles are usually comfortable, even tickled, when dealing with sizable numbers of people. The exalted roles like working with economy-size amounts of energy, large groups of people and broad ideas and concepts. They will stand out, often even with their looks. This planet has, by design, many fewer people in exalted roles than in the ordinal roles.

ARTISANS

Let's start with the role who's job it is to invent and create all change on the planet. If they are not masking themselves, Artisans are so light and diffuse you feel immediately their lack of specific gravity, that they are not attached to their bodies in a "feet solidly on the ground" sort of way.

Artisans are so immensely creative, they are usually pretty cute themselves. They often look a bit more loosely wired than the rest of us—Einstein is a perfect example of that—but there is also a very staunch core to Artisans. To think of them as fluff-balls is a grave error.

Their whole existence is creativity, from the biggest of inventions and discoveries to the creation of pleasant (or oppressive) moods in a room. Spontaneous and innovative, their creativity is not just physical, but philosophical, aesthetic, and atmospheric. You find Artisans everywhere (30% of our country's population) doing interesting, creative things—often in interesting, creative clothes.

Artisans are so fluid and decentralized that they can concentrate on five diverse things at a time. They will often have many projects going, to an extent that would frazzle the other roles. Aside from being sensitive types that often prefer to avoid crowds, Artisans need time alone, especially when they are into their creativity. They can forget friends or family exist, though it is not really a shunning; it is simply that they are so many eons away that the world almost does cease to exist.

With Artisans we are not just talking artists, inventors, actors, investigative scientists, engineers and mathematicians. Think about fix-it people, car repairpeople, craftspeople of all kinds, knitters and sewers, bakers, chefs, and women who create in a kitchen firmly under their control. Artisans thrive best with their own space, at least a room, where no one else touches a thing or interrupts.

Excitement to an Artisan is creation—which never stops—even after a work is complete. A person who sees fifty ways her successful play or skyscraper could have been improved on, may be embarassed by it now. Artisans invent everything new: from this year's trendiest furniture

41

fabrics to the non-caloric blueberry-Danish mouth-spray (for dieters) to the car that soothingly talks to you. In an Artisan home, furniture and other household items won't usually stay in the same old place for long. Artisans make rules about how things are and then invent great reasons why the rules don't apply in this case. Very clever people.

Because they are so quick, incessantly creative and sometimes chaos-producing, they are often misunderstood by the other roles and thus tend to gather into communities with each other. Gay men's communities are often full of Artisans, as is California's Silicon Valley with its thousands of computer designers and programmers. Whether it's actors, camerapeople, writers, sound effects, special effects, costume or makeup people, Hollywood is hog-heaven for Artisans.

Each of the roles has a positive and negative pole. For Artisans, the positive is creation and the negative pole, artifice or deception. Because Artisans are always creating and re-creating reality in their minds, their view of reality sometimes gets skewed, and they end up in a fantasy world, creatively pulling the wool over their own eyes. Deception and self-deception are something Artisans end up dealing with as part of the self-karma which goes with their territory.

There are many, many male Artisans currently in the United States which, by sheer virtue of numbers, has made the more "feminine" creative qualities somewhat culturally acceptable for men. It is much easier to be a male Artisan—a Paul McCartney or a Stephen Spielberg— now than it was in the decades prior to the seventies when sons were not to be ballet dancers or poets, florists or decorators, designers or artists and on and on. Of the Artisans now being born in the United States, three-fourths of them are male children; male sensitivity and creativity are definitely on a long term upswing.

Painters Gauguin, Van Gogh, Monet, Renoir, Maxfield Parrish, Andy Worhol and William Blake were all

Artisans, as are Entertainers Shirley MacLaine, Elizabeth Taylor, Candice Bergen, Meryl Streep, Molly Ringwald, River Phoenix, and Musicians Boy George, David Bowie, Elvis Presley, Bob Marley, Andreas Vollenweider, Liberace, Michael Jackson, and Mozart. *The Far Side's* Cartoonist, Gary Larson, and the immensely creative Walt Disney are in categories of their own. Film directors Woody Allen and George Lucas are both Artisans, as is former surgeon, current cosmetic company executive, Dr. Christian Barnard. Artisans Nikola Tesla and Albert Einstein were perhaps two of the most creative scientists of this century.

SAGES

Sages love collecting and sharing information, knowledge, and when you're lucky, wisdom. Their greatest desire is to make sure information is communicated clearly and disseminated to every part of the population that needs to hear it. This is what they put their hearts and passion into. They don't push too much to make sure you use their information. What's important to them is teaching, keeping it as light as possible. What's upsetting is miscommunication.

The Sage is perceptive, gifted at speaking, writing, and comic relief, creatively using words to put the language together in a unique and unusual way. Sages make sure the other roles know what all the others are thinking and feeling. They work more with feeling and emotion than intellectual constructs.

Friendly and colorful, Sages love to be the center of attention and are fufilled by it. You'll find them hogging it wherever possible; though because they only account for about 8% of our population, there is some room left for the the other six roles. They gather in communication centers like Los Angeles and Hollywood, the Bay Area and Silicon

Valley, and in New York, boosting Sage populations in those areas to 15%.

Because Sages are so pro good-times, they are often the slowest to mature into their true soul age each lifetime. Optimistic and light hearted, they try, by example, to show that a person can have fun and handle life too. They add spice wherever they are. They excel at cheering people even in stressful situations. This can be an important example for others; spirituality is not supposed to be a dreary giving up of life's goodies, and Sages know that intuitively.

The positive pole for Sages is expression, and the negative, oration. Oration means long-winded, droning on and on just to be talking and who cares how alive the content. This is the motor-mouth that people back away from.

Sages can top all the other roles in magnifying and overtelling some problem in their lives—or yours—milking it for *everything*. Because Sages excel with words, they have the potential for bending the truth to their favor without giving themselves away as easily as the other roles. It is important for them to know what the truth is, and they may stretch it. Part of this is the pleasure they take in choosing words that overemphasize, exaggerate and intensify to add to the dramatic or comedic value of what is being said.

Because they reach people through the powerful emotional center, no one can beat a Sage at the charisma game. You'll often find vibrant good looks, and with different cultures and soul levels, flash, glitter, plaid suits, used car salespeople, funny dope-heads, TV reporters, gossipers, actors, entertainers, preachers, comedians, teachers, political leaders, public speakers, media experts, hucksters, volunteers to be M.C., jokers, dirty jokers, clowns, class pests, and the shiniest of rock stars.

In the world in general, a good proportion of famous people are Sages. Some who have grabbed the public eye through politics are Ronald Reagan, Mikhail Gorbachev, Corazon Aquino, Robert Kennedy, and Harry Truman. It shouldn't suprise you to learn that TV's top four journalists, Dan Rather, Tom Brokaw, Peter Jennings and Mike Wallace are Sages doing their thing—disseminating information.

You may also add authors Stephen King, Norman Mailer, James Michner, Truman Capote, Ken Kesey, Farley Mowat, Alice Walker, Dr. Ruth Westheimer—and Shakespeare to your list of Sages.

Sage actors include Richard Burton, Michael J. Fox, William Hurt, William Shatner, Richard Chamberlain, and Harrison Ford. Sages rarely pop up as the actresses who gain public affection. Our culture seems to prefer the inspirational qualities of the Priest or the softness of the Artisan woman to the brash earthiness of the Sage. It's more difficult for an audience to project feelings onto a Sage because she is so blatantly herself.

Here's a shortened list of comics who all "just happen" to be Sages: Sammy Davis, Jr., Johnny Carson, Richard Pryor, Billy Crystal, Chevy Chase, Eddie Murphy, Lennie Bruce, Milton Berle, George Burns, Bette Midler, Whoopi Goldberg and Jane Dornacker. Luciano Pavarotti, Frank Sinatra, Buddy Holly, Mick Jagger and Sting are all entertaining Sage-brand singers. Timothy Leary, now busy at work on computer games to enhance self-communication, seems to be in his very own Sage category. Carmen Miranda was a very expressive Sage exhibiting much creative Artisan (fruit on the head) influence. Are you getting the gist of how it is that Sages serve the other roles?

Werner Erhard, Rajneesh, Satchidananda, and Muktnanda are some spiritual teachers with that special Sage flavor.

SERVERS

Servers are so nice to be around that it is a shame there are no longer 30% here in the United States. It's down to barely 10% overall and worse on the two coasts. This creates a less neighborly, more callous, cynical atmosphere. But the good news is that they are now being born back into our culture at about the former rate.

Many Servers live in China where their role is venerated. They chose China both to help push that country forward and as a way to help the country take the long view of the common good. Their current proportion in that population is a whopping 50%. Most of the time we all prefer to be in places where our role (and chosen sex) is respected. (Sometimes we go for the hard lessons; we may be paying back karma by taking a look at a situation which has been reversed so it is no longer in our "favor").

With our predominant Western philosophy of every man and woman for him or herself, the last couple decades in the United States have not glorified self-sacrifice nor the virtues of the little woman behind the big man. However, with the influence of the Servers now starting to be born in their former proportions in the U.S. again, family life should start to look more promising, and the divorce rate should plummet. The society will feel softer and there's a better chance all those Baby Boomers will be taken care of in their old age. We need those Servers, and they know it.

We've all likely had a Server mother or special Server grandparent, or known regret for what we missed. Servers do put other's needs before their own. They truly like to help out and will do almost anything for anyone. Servers nurture both people and space, making home (and office) environments feel really good too.

While they are often sweet, Servers are not routinely warm emotionally. They show you their love by what they do for you, not necessarily by making an emotional connection. Servers usually display sweetness in their eyes and have a feeling of receptivity in their bodies. However, they are not open to information that would put their lives in flux; they hold stability as an important value.

Until very recently, the Server role is exactly what

women around the world were expected to be. This training was so strong that older women now often look like Servers—sweet, behind the scenes people dressed in nice neutral colors—and are <u>anything</u> <u>but</u> in actuality.

A stable, inspirational role that prefers to stay in the background, they give people the support that allows things to happen. Phil Donahue, running around with that microphone so everybody gets a chance to speak, is a terrific example of a Server who loves to be of service in that modest, self-effacing kind of way Server's have.

Sometimes reluctant to confront people or even ask questions that might attract attention, these are not self-starters nor idea people, rather they are best carrying out other's ideas.

Server's can also weave intricate webs, covertly manipulating by creating guilt through their very givingness. Part of the Servers' self-karma may be a tendency to enslave themselves to a cause, a wife or husband, a sick person or a boss. Or people may resist their serving out of resentment for the manipulation that may be underneath all the goodies.

In Infant and Baby times they'll raise large families, take care of farms and animals, and sign up for wars to help their country. Later stages still find them creating families of size and going for service occupations, whether barber or bus driver, teacher or waiter, midwife, healer or doctor, or benevolent humanistic scientist. They very much like to feel useful and enjoy making people around them feel well taken care of. They, therefore, typically have lives blessed by many close family ties and people who care for them.

You'll find them in support positions for causes they want to push. Since Servers aren't usually comfortable with leadership positions, you won't find as many rising to prominence as any of the other roles, and the ones who do are usually noted for being of exceptional service to a cause. They want their service, not themselves, to shine.

Dian Fossey spent 18 years living with, studying and

caring for gorillas in central Africa. Other Servers are Mrs. See of See's Candy, Mother Teresa, Florence Nightingale, Albert Schweitzer, Bob Geldof (Live Aid), Martin Luther King, Jr., Winnie Mandela, Bishop Tutu, Deng Xiaoping, Queen Victoria, Queen Elizabeth, Prince Charles, and Jimmy Carter. You'll notice, even among famous Servers, the general inclination not to grab the center stage, a tendency which caused political problems for President Carter. Media-permeated America runs on the stimulus of dynamism, verve, and charisma. It is difficult for a Server to both be true to his or her essence and have the desire and willingness to take the spotlight in such a showy way.

PRIESTS

Energetic, very powerful people, Priests are in high demand as inspirers and facilitators of spiritual growth. We owe them our utopian visions, rituals and ceremonies and even most of the meditations which utilize visualization. They are masters with symbols. Natural leaders of causes, Priests are plucky, inspirational types who get us unafraid and optimistic about making changes, both in ourselves and our world.

This is the most high frequency and intense of the roles. Priests grow faster, even tending to cycle off with many fewer lives, than the rest of us. Extra light and a glint in the eye is the easy way to spot the 3 to 4% of our population who are Priests. A very loving compassion is another indication—and is the positive pole of Priest. The unity of all creation is a living fact for them; they know the physical plane is a mere part of the show.

Zeal is the negative pole and can mean there is such a strong inclination towards inspiring others that Priests aren't always interested in whether their information is either accurate or desired. And since they are so quick and energetic, they may zealously poke and badger the rest of us, "Grow faster," they say. "Wake up!!!" For this hammering away, they sometimes earn a reputation as tough to be around.

Rapid in their thinking, often impulsive, Priests have a sense of mission and purpose which is idealistic, heading towards the visionary and perhaps the impossibly impractical. They may joke around a bit, but then bring the conversation around to a subject more elevated, one they feel is important, usually for you. Enthusiastic Priests will happily talk for extended periods on how people can improve their lives. They are always reaching and encourage others to reach. Priests, who can inspire themselves even in difficult situations, don't easily understand how others can wallow for periods without self-motivation.

The role of Priest is the most difficult role to handle appropriately. The tendency to be a buzzy, high frequency types, plus the overriding desire to push for people's spiritual welfare, may make them too hasty, unreasoning and impromptu. Their remarks as well as their projects may show up as ill-considered.

They may be involved in numbers of projects with an intensity which would cause burnout among the rest of us. It does in them too, just not as quickly. As an exalted role, like Sages and Kings, Priests are skilled in communicating with large groups and tend to prefer that as a way of working over one-to-one interactions. They do carry banners. More time is likely to be spent with causes than relationships.

Priests are given towards service specifically aimed at the spiritual side of a human being. Utilizing their deep compassion, they make excellent healers on physical as well as spiritual levels. Priests are often attracted to roles in the clergy and can also make excellent therapists. They like to be anywhere they can have an influence and inspire others toward a greater vision. This often includes politics.

Telling examples of famous Priests, who range from

inspirational to zealous, are Carl Jung, Thomas Aquinas, Joan of Arc, Ayn Rand, Terry Cole-Whittaker, John Lilly of dolphin fame, and author Lynn Andrews *(Medicine Woman)*. California's Rose Bird's zealous compassion towards criminals lost her her job as Chief Justice. Nancy Reagan ("Just say no!"), Coretta Scott King, Pat Robertson, Tom Hayden, Jesse Jackson, and Moammar Khadafy are several more Priests from the political front. Princess Diana, Lily Tomlin, Debra Winger, Thomas Dolby, Bob Dylan, Stevie Wonder, J.S. Bach and Allen Ginsberg round out the picture. Princess Diana seems to be waking up her prince, while all the others aim(ed) to wake up the rest of us.

WARRIORS

A very solid role, at the opposite end of the frequency scale from the zingy Priest. Warriors are slow and steady in the pursuit of their goals and targets. They usually have clear objectives, purposes and principles which they hold dear. Determined in terms of action, superb at strategy and tactics, Warriors tend to be so focused on do, do, do, that they may lack breadth of vision until their Old Soul lifetimes.

They are the most physical role, choosing strong bodies and living life through their five senses. They are happy on the physical plane, strongly appreciating sex, food and sports. They usually take on many more lives than the rest of us and use more time to cycle-off. Unlike Priests, they see no hurry.

Warriors are the ones who create social structure, social institutions, order and civilization *and* the space for Artisans to create culture. They set up banking systems, school systems, health care and welfare systems, and then go about enforcing all the rules.

Since most Warriors like independence and need to

feel they are winning their own battles, you don't find them using the welfare system they so carefully constructed, even when they could legitimately be there. They would also much rather earn their own money than have lottery winnings fall into their lap. Not earning their own way puts Warriors in conflict with the principles which are truly at the heart of their being.

In early lives, Warriors actually go for physical battles and lives of mayhem and violence as soldiers, robbers, pirates, raiders of other tribes, gang fighters, and so on, using whatever drama is available to gain experience. This is not to say that the rest of us don't do these things, just that the draw for Warriors is much stronger.

From the mid-Baby to mid-Mature parts of the cycle, they will head in large numbers for police departments, the armed services, the FBI and CIA, the Pentagon, college and professional football, wrestling, various martial arts, and to the top of large corporations in blue pin-striped battle suits, or into politics with principles, purpose and those incredible organizational abilities in tow.

Warriors value practicality and principles much more than aesthetics. If their large dog digs up your flower bed, they may have a difficult time understanding your emotional distress; after all they cemented over their back yard to make one big practical patio years ago. When go-getter Warriors become real estate developers, each house may end up the same practical style and color. From aesthetics to efficiency, MacDonald's and other fast food chains bear a strong Warrior influence.

Becoming a doctor is popular among late Baby Soul Warriors as a way of getting out of mayhem and chaos by learning to take care of people in a structured way, while many Young Souls use skillful doctoring as an excellent method of paying back karma they've incurred on the battlefield.

In later lives, Warriors, who often even look a little bristly, have to deal with the ingrained tendency toward violence and root it out. Overt, blatant, and unsubtle, Warriors are not superb communicators and can lapse right into coercion (their negative pole) or intimidation when frustrated. Compromise and give-and-take are their strong suit. Not being great communicators generally makes Warriors the poorest of liars. This, along with their principles, tends to keep them honest.

Warriors can be ruthless, bullying, narrow-minded, hot-tempered and unforgiving, as well as productive, protecting, grounded, reliable, practical people who make swell parents.

There are currently 30% Warriors in the United States, three-quarters of them now incarnating as women. This pushes women forward into new fields with levels of competence surprising to many. These forthright Warrior women help make strong, highly organized women acceptable in our society and corporations, in much the same way the large numbers of Artisan males have made sensitivity more acceptable in men.

Geraldine Ferraro is a Warrior who forged ahead into very new territory as a woman. Mary Kay Ash formed a cosmetic empire, Christie Hefner is running Playboy Enterprises and Joan Rivers nipping at the ratings of (Sage) Johnny Carson, while Princess Stephanie shocks with her boyish punk look and tattoo. Warrior women are everyplace, changing everything.

General Patton, L. Ron Hubbard, George Shultz, Clint Eastwood, Paul Volcker, Henry Kissinger, Ed Zschau, Grace Jones, and Golda Meier are Warriors obvious almost by looks alone, while Ralph Nader and Jane Fonda are obvious by their high principles, organizational abilities and willingness to take on tough battles.

Worldwide, Warriors rise to the top as political leaders, elected or otherwise: examples are Bismark, Churchill, Ferdinand Marcos, Baby Doc Duvalier, George Wallace, Miguel de la Madrid (Mexico), Ayatollah

Khomeini and a good percentage of the tough military leaders, like Chile's Pinochet, who run third world countries.

The United States has many fewer Warrior politicians these days because the job requires enormous subtlety and adroitness to survive the media exposure. Straight-shooting Eisenhower was our last Warrior president back in the simpler decade of the fifties.

Warriors produce spiritual teachers too. Yogi Bhajan of the Sikhs is a powerful Old Warrior. Ken Keyes is the Warrior who organized Buddhism into a step-by-step program for busy Americans in his *Handbook to Higher Consciousness* and then went on to provide a backbone of support to the now burgeoning peace movement with *The Hundreth Monkey* .

Mohammed Ali is an example of a sports figure with a powerful Warrior body. Warriors who become actors—like Rock Hudson, Sylvester Stallone, Charlton Heston or even Robert Redford—are usually better known as "hunks" than as superb actors. Warriors who become actresses—like Marilyn Monroe, Mae West and Joan Collins—may be more acknowledged for their blatant sexuality than their acting skills, though Warrior Jane Fonda has received tribute for both. Powerhouse Mary Lou Retton, a hunk in her own way, is another example of the Warrior at work.

Ernest Hemingway and Gertrude Stein are excellent examples of the non-flowery Warrior writing style. Richard Wagner was a Warrior who took on music—and put battle scenes into his operas. Jim Morrison, Tina Turner and Rod Stewart, along with a good percentage of other hard-driving rock musicians, are Warriors.

KINGS

The King is oriented towards seeking mastery in every situation. Attempting to be able to learn very quickly and become expert at almost anything encountered is par for the King course. It is a difficult role requiring perseverence and self-direction, and since only 1% of our population is Kings, there are few role models for emulation. They will tell you that their throne easily becomes the hot seat.

Kings, when they are children, are usually frustrated in their rush towards mastery and can become quite tyranical (negative pole) because of the difficult uphill work they choose. They want to be competent (perfectionists) in all they do, whether it is tying shoes, vying for school grades, or succeeding in team sports.

Just as every Artisan is not an artist, every King does not have an empire. Kings do, however tend to command respect. They like large powerful bodies, preferably male, so their presence draws attention even more easily. Unbothered by timidity, they know their worth and place; they know they are Kings.

Although they incline towards big egos and arrogance—which is a part of their self-karma—they are natural leaders who attract much allegiance. They can display a very gentle benevolence. Unlike the narrowly focused Warrior, they can easily see the whole picture, so people instinctively trust their advice.

Upright and reputable for the most part, they tend to rise to the top early in life, becoming managers and delegators of authority, whether in a pizza restaurant or a warehouse, as the head of a corporation or a country, or as a judge or politician.

Kings look more exalted and refined than the Warriors and often exude a steely, regal bearing; that they know they are Kings shows. They may disguise this, but at their core you can feel they know themselves to be the final authority in their universe. Frequently charismatic and commanding, they inspire loyalty and devotion in people around them.

The Michael entity is composed primarily of Warriors and Kings, giving it a practical, highly organized flavor as well as a strong drive toward mastery. Delegation may be a strong suit too considering how many Michael channels are out and about.

America's best shot at royalty, John and Jacqueline Kennedy, were both Kings. Tycoons Aristotle Onassis, William Randolph Hearst and J. Paul Getty are also Kings. Former CIA Director William Casey was a King doing a typical job—running a powerful organization. The CEO's of many huge organizations including Safeway, ARCO, ABC, CBS and The Limited are Kings.

Otto Preminger, Orson Wells, Alec Guinness, John Forsythe, Diahann Carroll, Madonna and Katherine Hepburn are examples from the Hollywood scene. John Muir, Alexander the Great, Haile Selassie, King of Ethiopia, and Prince Michael of Greece are others, as is Rama, a spiritual teacher in the Southern California area and Betty Bethards, a psychic and spiritual teacher in Northern California.

SCHOLARS

Their job is to take careful note of everything that exists and bring all the information back to their entiity and ultimately to the Akashic records. Compelled from within to gather and assimilate knowledge, their curiosity is a driving force. Thorough and detail oriented, all information is relevant to the Scholar. Needing to take time to see how this universe works, nuts and bolts, makes them one of the slower roles to finish this physical plane game.

Scholars are a very neutral 10% of us. In fact, they are difficult to spot unless you remember to look for their neutrality and their unusually large foreheads as clues.

Because they are so absorbtive, there is a quietness to them. They graze unobtrusively for knowledge wherever they are, though their eyes may be bulging if they are really interested.

They usually aren't overtly expressive and may look a little reserved occasionally, sometimes seeming to be spectators of life. Customarily dressing in neutrals to better blend with the woodwork, they don't like being pulled off-center, either into the spotlight (for the most part) or into unrestrained anger or joy. They don't freely express feelings, but will usually give out that information when asked.

You see Servers wanting to give, Sages acting up, Artisans creating or dreaming, Priests cajoling, Warriors and Kings busy doing or directing, and Scholars staring or nodding their head as they assimilate some particular tidbit of information. As the neutral role, they help the other roles connect with and understand each other.

Scholars are a solid, grounded role; when they are around, their presence allows the other roles to more easily communicate. They are like the neutral hub-of-the-wheel for the rest of us and thus can make excellent mediators and counselors for others, seeing all sides of a situation objectively. Scholars are often able to react neutrally to situations that would bring disturbed emotions flying out of the rest of us.

Scholars are oriented toward the accumulation of knowledge but not necessarily for communication or dissemination. They store information, sometimes to the detriment of their innately strong bodies. Certain Scholars happily study every facet possible of one single insect, or one single point in history—for a lifetime. They may be philosophers, scientists or historians who are happy in academia with the increased access to information, but Scholars can be anyplace studying *anything* and don't necessarily put their nose in a book to do it. They still double-check their facts. When they seek adventure, it is out of an avid curiosity to know more. "What is over the next hill?" "What would happen if I added some wings and jumped?"

Observing, thorough, understanding, integrating, and logical, this is the Scholar in the positive pole. In the negative pole, an individual may be too speculative, theoretical and intellectualizing, spinning endless probabilities around in the brain. A Scholar may be so bland on the exterior that people don't pay much attention to her, and even further out on the negative side, she may be a reclusive, dull and dusty museum piece.

The Scholars who go for political roles will often be the types who are conscious of history. George Washington exemplifies this, as does Richard Nixon, walking off the plane into China and history. Chairman Mao, Margaret Thatcher, Daniel Ortega, Teddy Kennedy and P.W. Botha are other Scholar-politicians. Note the neutral overall quality to these people, particularly telling considering they are all "on stage".

Other examples of Scholars are Heraclites, Galileo, Mormon Joseph Smith, poet Stephen Spender, whiz kid Steven Jobs, naturalist and author Edward Abbey. Beethoven and Aaron Copland are both Scholars. TV's Mr. Rogers ("What do you think would happen if we ....?") is a Scholar, as is the even more eccentric PeeWee Herman. Football player William "Refrigerator" Perry has both the even disposition and solid body of the Scholar.

The extraordinarily steadfast Anatoly Shcharansky is a Scholar who just emerged from nine years of "study" in the Gulag prison camps. Ouspensky was the Scholar who rather dryly preserved Gurdjieff's teachings. Margaret Mead, Admiral Perry and Carlos Castaneda were three Scholars bent on adventure while compiling their new knowledge. And let's not forget P.M. Roget who put English into the myriad cross-referenced categories found in the handy thesaurus still usually bearing his name.

CHAPTER FIVE
THE PERSONALITY OVERLEAVES

The *overleaves* are personality traits which overlay a person's core or essence each lifetime, enabling the essence to create and play a different character on the new stage each lifetime presents. These varying personality traits facilitate lessons the essence is set on learning in a given lifetime.

By screening and distorting the essence's own purer energy, the overleaves introduce variety, color and richness into our lives. We can challenge ourselves with difficult traits, lead with dynamic ones, kick back with easy ones—or run around in circles with overleaves pulling us in several directions at once.

Knowledge of our own overleaves helps to show where we are on the map of all possible ways of being human. Again, like the roles, when we know which overleaves are ours, the ability to relax and go with the flow expands.

Consciously working to stay in the positive pole of those overleaves which cause us difficulty has great practical value—since it is the only way growth happens. Contrary to certain cultural beliefs, growth does not occur as long as we are wallowing in the negative corners of our personalities. Aside from the pain, all that suffering does not amount to much more than a reminder to change our ways.

The overleaves are organized to include a **goal** for each lifetime; a **mode,** which is the method of going after the goal—and life in general; an **attitude,** which is the way we look at things; and a **chief negative feature,** the stumbling block which makes living really interesting (read: more difficult). As with the roles, the overleaves are oriented toward expression, inspiration, action or assimilation.

Knowing our own personality's overleaves helps us be clearer about our individuality. Discovering other people's overleaves helps us be clearer and kinder about their individuality and their differences from us. Knowing what is going on makes tolerance, acceptance and love all easier. That is the point.

GOALS

The goal chosen each lifetime is the strongest indication of what the essence aims to achieve in that life. The goal is actually the bottom line issue in every experience during a lifetime, conscious or not. Life situations will tend to bring us face to face with our goals so that we continually research and examine those issues.

Stay in the positive pole of your goal in every experience, and your essence will be turning cartwheels—though you might be bored having your life flow so smoothly. Set out to catch yourself, red-handed, in the negative pole of your goal (or any other overleaf), and you set out to create a happier, growing person. Promises, promises. . .

Some overleaves are chosen infrequently because they confine experience to such narrow bounds—or simply because they are very troublesome. Eventually, though, every essence gains practical, hands-on knowledge of each of the overleaves.

The percentages shown after the overleaves refer to the number of people taking on that particular trait at any one time, and by extension the average number of your lifetimes spent within that personality atmosphere. So, if you are doing a lifetime in *discrimination,* that critical mind you think so integral to your unique specialness is probably only yours, to such a degree, in a mere 2% of your lifetimes.

Discrimination—2%
Expression axis

Chosen often after lifetimes of overly-accepting doormat-hood for the purpose of eliminating from one's life what is not wanted. Discrimination bestows the needed backbone to convert from being mushy. These selective people are expressive and will tell you their opinions and why they are justified in holding them.

In the positive pole, discrimination creates worldly refinement, discernment, sophistication, excellent critical faculties, and pride in savoring only the best in life.

The negative may cause people to become snobby if not categorically rejecting. Never satisfied, they may be picky hairsplitters and so judgmental, aloof, and prejudiced that they drive others from them. This much negativity is not a lot of fun to be around.

A sample of people using discrimination: Fred Astaire, David Byrne, Bob Dylan, Richard Gere, Orson Welles, Steven Jobs, Michele Duvalier and TV Newswoman Suzanne Saunders; also many authors, critics and reviewers; comics, detective heroes, decorators, dancers, chefs, and tea, coffee, wine and chocolate tasters.

Acceptance—30%
Expression axis

The big issue is accepting life and the people in it. Often a big issue is desiring and gaining acceptance from others, or at the very least, not getting rejected.

People in acceptance display lighthearted good spirits; you find in their eyes softness and approachability, for they are botching it if they aren't "accepting" you.

Very popular with Old Souls, acceptance is the most "spiritual" of the goals and the most wonderful to accomplish. It is where we are all heading.

In the positive pole you find warm, understanding, agreeable, self-accepting, friendly people. They may be experiencing the a higher state of loving energy, what Michael calls agape. It can look like bliss; it can create humanitarianism and philanthropy.

In the negative pole, people using acceptance become ingratiating, insincere, and way too fearful of rejection.

They lose themselves to niceness and flattery. On an inner level they may not be in touch with what they want or be able to make the discriminations which would help steer their lives.

These are political figures with acceptance as their goal: John F. Kennedy, Ronald Reagan, Bishop Tutu, Corazon Aquino, and Peru's President, Alan Garcia. "Dynasty's" inspirationally nice actress, Linda Evans, has acceptance as a goal as do Robert Redford, Woody Allen, Stevie Wonder, Robin Williams and Alice Walker. Swami Chidvilasananda and Ram Dass are two spiritual teachers who deal with acceptance issues. Can you help but notice the approachable, nice-guy quality in each of these people?

Re-evaluation —1%
Inspiration axis

Re-evaluation limits the scope of life so that one or more major issues may be fully examined. These are issues avoided in so many past lives that the person finally gives a full lifetime to what has been buried deeply in the instinctive center.

People are not usually consciously looking at issues here, but ruminating or brooding without a clear focus. Issues are often so deeply buried that they are difficult to clarify even with channeling. It is as if the person has managed to obscure the information even in the Akashic Records.

This is not an easy catch-up to accomplish; it is uncomfortable and self-limiting. In fact, many who are autistic, retarded or brain-damaged are living lives with the goal of re-evaluation.

In the positive pole these people display simplicity and reduced distractions. Under the surface, they are inspecting, reviewing, contemplating, and consolidating. They may feel unassuming and a little artless to others.

The negative pole tends to be a stuck, bewildered, withdrawn sort of a place. Greatly internalized, a person in re-evaluation may not be completely "here".

Because of the nature of this goal, it seemed it would be difficult to find many who were famous. The suprise was easily finding a handful of people using this goal and making a splash in the world. They are the cigar-chomping head of the Federal Reserve, Paul Volcker, Secretary of State George Shultz, Alabama's George Wallace, Anatoly Shcharansky, and authors Edward Abbey and Stephen King.

Growth—40%
Inspiration axis

To choose this goal is to choose a whirlwind lifetime with an inner desire pushing you to gain new experience, constantly, with little time for rest and recuperation or assimilation. Life may look like a never-ending series of challenges and obstacles to deal with and overcome, or so full of desired experiences that it's nearly impossible to choose. Growth, the fundamental characteristic of the universe, is gained—with dispatch.

People with this goal have their hands full; they feel driven to take on new experiences and thus create busy lives. They choose what to do not on the basis of "Is it fun?" or "Is this a good career move?" but on whether the experience will further growth and development. Choosing this way is very essence-directed. Since rest seems an anathema, they understandably look a bit tired underneath all the glowing enthusiasm.

It may be that the man who has taken growth workshops forever and still won't listen to your feelings, is a person with a goal of growth, for his own challenges will typically take priority over other people's needs or feelings. He will love to talk about what he has done and what it means.

In the positive pole you see outgoing eagerness, tremendous activity, many experiences and, ultimately, evolution. Meeting challenges may create satisfaction, clarity and . . . growth.

In the negative pole, growth causes people to exhibit confusion and absent mindedness, and to manifest complications like you wouldn't believe. Driven, self-oriented, they may be callous to the needs of others. When they finally rest by slipping into re-evaluation, they cover themselves as best they can, not admitting, even to themselves, that they needed a break.

Examples of people who make their lives hum and spin in this way are Robert Kennedy, Jesse Jackson, Phil Donahue, Louis Rukeyser, Carlos Castaneda, Whoopi Goldberg, Dustin Hoffman, Pee-Wee Herman, Bette Midler, Norman Mailer and Farley Mowat.

Submission —10%
Action axis

This goal creates a personality very sensitive to the needs of others. It is chosen sometimes in order to pull a person away from lifetimes of self-centered arrogance. Servers use this goal infrequently because it is similar to what they are about anyway.

Submission lifetimes often entail a search to find appropriate people, groups or ideas to devote oneself to because fufillment (of this goal) is found through activity which serves desired ideals. Religious orders and gurus, environmental issues, and the full spectrum of political causes from peace to minority rights solicit attention from many in submission.

They feel waylaid if an appropriate cause to undertake or person to attend to hasn't been found, so these dedicated types usually have their antennae up for valuable causes or people to serve—even while they are engrossed in something else.

In the positive pole, submission inclines one to stay busy serving people, ideas or causes selflessly. One key to the positive pole seems to be having *appropriate* people or ideas to be immersed in. This way a person can experience some payoffs for all the gung-ho devotion and attention he or she quite happily puts out.

Slipping into the negative pole to only a minor degree, a person might feel vaguely unworthy when temporarily out of a cause. Deeper in, the negative pole cooks up behaviors like obedience, dutifulness, and unthinking compliance, so that a person becomes subservient and resigned. Feelings of being victimized, even enslaved or martyred, arise in people no longer feeling in charge of their lives.

Because submission encourages people to become devoted to a goal, there are plenty of famous examples to choose from. How about Ralph Nader? Or Jane Fonda? Dian Fossey? Or Pope John Paul II and Mother Teresa? Francis Moore Lappe has worked for nearly 20 years to get this "small planet" healthy and fed. Terry Cole-Whittaker is an example of a spiritual teacher who puts herself behind her ideals. Our Nancy Reagan devotes herself tirelessly to her husband and his goals as well as to her own "Just say no to drugs!" campaign. China's Deng Xioping devotes himself to changing the economic base of his country. Television's perserving Mr. Rogers devotes himself to helping children discover how the world works. You'll notice in this group a sampling of the diverse goals people choose to serve: the poor, the dying, the hungry, children, animals, peace, God, and "your good"—be it your prosperity or health, product safety or your political environment.

Dominance -10%
Action axis

Individuals in dominance always have energy to gain the upper hand on what situations life brings their way. They want the reins in their hands, even as a child. This goal creates natural leaders who prevail by creating win-win situations; that way people feel comfortable following.

Dominance in our language takes on pejorative connotations. With Michael's use of the word, dominance is a quality others rate highly—when it is being used appropriately—because it is pretty nice to let others handle some things for us. "Sure, go ahead, make a decision on that. Let me know what you do."

The problem in being around someone in dominance comes with not setting limits; for if a person in dominance senses a void, he or she jumps immediately to fill it. It is natural; dominance can't help but desire to control.

In the positive pole these energetic people are determined, capable leaders who rise easily to the top. They are in charge of their lives, cut a wide swath in the world, and are usually appreciated and listened to.

In the negative pole you may find a dictatorial, demanding, overwhelming, overbearing, insensitive, controlling person that everyone avoids whenever feasible. This person is not creating the win-win situations dominance is justly famous for, but practicing winner-take-all and losing in the process. Because people in dominance want to dominate, they don't usually wallow in the ineffective negative pole too long.

Illustrations of the goal are found in the lives and personalities of George Washington, Ferdinand Marcos, Henry Kissinger, Mikhail Gorbachev, Pat Robertson, Khomeini, Madonna, Sean Penn, Grace Jones, Sylvester Stallone, Mae West, Katherine Hepburn, Elizabeth Taylor, J.Paul Getty, Mary Kay Ash, Jeremy Rifkin, and Richard

Ramirez. Each, in his or her own way, is a very strong character intent on living according to his or her own plan. Good luck to Madonna and Sean.

Stagnation —7%
Assimilation axis

This is often a person recuperating from a trying bunch of lives. Stagnation, like dominance or submission, is not a dirty word. The purpose of a stagnation lifetime is rest—while learning to go with the flow.

Stagnation lifetimes are not set up to contain many challenges or intense activity. Smooth sailing should come easily. If people learn how to go with the current, they will get what they want fairly effortlessly; if not, they struggle around, don't get what they want, and they don't get rest either.

In the positive pole these people look free-flowing, unstressed, and rested. They coast and glide and are rather pleased with themselves. Life exists here without much drama; they are not seeking to shape events and therefore know a tranquility which escapes their more driven cousins.

In the negative pole, stagnation may look inert, lazy, and uncommitted; or you'll see them with enough (manmade) struggles and worry that they thrash about going against the current. And they are tired.

Fame brings strain, so examples are obviously scarce in the famous department, but there is author Margaret Atwood, artist Georgia O'Keefe, and football player "Refrigerator" Perry. All three seem to have lives and careers that flow along pretty easily.

The neutral or assimilative goal of stagnation has the potential for "sliding" into the experiences of the other six goals, though usually one or two favorite landing spots are picked. A person might spend most of his time in stagnation, but bounce frequently into a loving, feel-good, acceptance place while alternatively going for dominance when there was a perceived need to make something happen.

Similarly, each of the goals easily slides to the one it is paired with, so a person in acceptance may develop great critical faculties or hate herself for being so picky when in the discrimination arena.

When you find yourself uncomfortably in the negative pole of your goal, the easiest way to end that behavior is to consciously go to the positive pole of the paired goal. Dominance and submission are paired; thus a man in dominance who finds himself getting dictatorial can most easily move out of that by choosing to serve someone selflessly in that moment, thereby using the positive pole of submission. Going to the opposite is an easier way out than struggling back into dominance's positive pole of leadership, while simultaneously letting go of the dictatorial element.

A person at the negative end of submission experiencing subservience and feeling victimized, would be advised to head for the positive side of dominance, leadership, where she could get the determination to move from exploitation towards taking control of her own life.

The man in growth who is Adam's-apple-deep in confusing experiences, could do with some temporary simplicity, which is the positive pole of re-evaluation, growth's paired goal. While not unusual to find "growth" people sitting eyes glazed, mouth open, in front of the TV, it is usually a little unclear if that is the positive pole of re-evaluation, simplicity, or the negative, withdrawal.

MODES

Modes are how we approach life, how we go after our goal (see above), as well as how we go after goals in their more conventional sense. It is the most visible of the overleaves; people notice this about you.

The mode is the method we most commonly use to make something happen, our most habitual way of approach (or avoidance). It is the way we live life whether it's *cautious, passionate,* or always *persevering.* The mode shows the kind of action we are prone to employing.

As with the goals, each of the paired modes will experiment at times with its opposite. A *power* mode person will know a fair amount about *caution,* often from the negative pole. A person who has the assimilative *observation* mode will slide around using all of the modes at times, but again having a few favored landing positions.

Michael's system is not rigid. Anyone can use any overleaf occasionally. The system does show what people's routine patterns and ways of acting are, which is advantageous whether you are looking at other people or at yourself.

Caution—20%
Expressive axis

Caution helps people approach life carefully and may be chosen to calm down past life tendencies to jump into entangling situations. As you can see, at 20% popularity, many think they need holding back. It is popular with Young and Baby Souls to help them stop being reactive to the circumstances life presents.

This is the constantly deliberating, always look-before-you-leap crowd. These are people who are wary in their approach to situations, worrying that something may go wrong. They don't want to regret their behavior. This caution is felt by observers and is a little contagious in that it may bring up other people's fears too.

In the positive pole, caution makes for safe and deliberate behavior. Risk-adverse, and quite careful about consequences, insurance probably gets paid on time and tires are watched for wear. You can count on a caution mode person to be tactful and diplomatic so as not to stir up trouble.

In the negative pole, caution mode people become irrationally fearful, very phobic and superstitious, not only afraid of walking under ladders, but afraid to leave home without 20 locks on the doors, a burglar alarm ready, charms in their pockets, protection prayers in their wallets and a full tank of gas. Masks anyone? Caution mode, from this side, can feel uncomfortably neurotic, pretty hopeless and stuck. It is difficult to even be able to decide to take an action.

Because of the nature of this overleaf, examples of people in public life do not abound, but you can see how caution affects the following four: George Washington, Secretary of Defense Caspar Weinberger, who is 100% convinced we need the protection of more weapons *and* Star Wars, horror story author Stephen King, and South Africa's Winnie Mandela, who has, probably wisely, been uneasy in the limelight caused by the imprisonment of her husband.

Caution mode tends towards self-blockage and is therefore self-karmic. Self-karmas are little (or big) lessons we give ourselves to play with to gain experience and keep life interesting. Power mode, caution's twin, is outgoing and easily karma creating.

Power —20%
Expressive Axis

You feel the presence of a power mode individual as he goes through his day by the confident stance he takes; power lends an air of authority that is unmissable. Power mode is more showy than dominance and more difficult for others to deal with. Dominance goes from one issue to the next, while power mode is more pervasive. The two are often used together to create a powerhouse personality.

In the positive pole, these outgoing people are authoritative, confident, influential and commanding. Their powerful presence stands out energetically and is noticed, as is their style, and approach.

In the negative pole, power makes others feel fearful; a power mode person may become insensitive, pushy and bullying. He may become highhanded and peremptory, qualities unappreciated by those around him. When not getting his way, the power mode individual can create a big black cloud those "thwarting" him will feel. However, a power mode person is usually are quite unconscious of being oppressive, sometimes even after it is pointed out, time and again.

Examples of a few who have gained fame with the help of power mode are Machiavelli, Robert F. Kennedy, Chairman Mao, L. Ron Hubbard, Dr. Christian Barnard, Jeremy Rifkin, Imelda and Ferdinand Marcos, Mikhail Gorbachev, Orson Welles, Madonna, Werner Erhard and Swami Chidvilasananda.

Repression—2%
Inspiration axis

Repression lifetimes are chosen to compensate for lifetimes of glut and excess or simply to learn to hold back, a bit like caution mode, but this time for the pursuit of internal sophistication and elegance. This mode requires individuals to find a way to express emotions politely, in as refined a manner as possible. Coarseness and lack of dignity will drive them quietly crazy. The withholding of emotion necessary here is very hard on both the expressive roles, Artisan and Sage.

In the positive pole, you see restraint, contained emotions, and tactful, civilized behavior. These people look like products of "good breeding"; they are disciplined, refined, polished. They likely display a connoisseur's taste and appreciation for beauty.

People using repression mode become noticeably inhibited and withheld in the negative pole. Cut off from their muffled emotions, they may be listless and blocked, seemingly without means to bring to light the real issues which bother and ultimately depress them. Others experience them as unresponsive, a little too cool with feelings.

Examples of people who have the kind of restrained tastefulness typical of this mode are Prince Charles, David Niven, Alec Guiness, Nancy Reagan, Mary Tyler Moore, David Byrne and Fred Astaire. There are occupations that draw people using repression mode right into their folds; gourmet cooking does, as does interior design, diplomacy, and classical dance and music. "Romance novel heroine" can't be said to be a profession, though the women depicted in that genre usually display the refinement and nicety common to the mode.

Passion —10%
Inspiration axis

People rarely take two lives in a row in passion mode. The tendency it gives is to impetuously lose oneself in the often intense actions and emotions of the moment. In making choices, these outgoing people go for what holds the most excitement and passion for them; they do not carefully weigh things out. Sometimes they do not weigh things out at all.

Because emotions are accentuated, passion mode is a favorite of Mature Souls. It gives a grand ability to enjoy the moment and energy to go after whatever it is that attracts attention or desire. The trick of staying positive is to maintain *some* sense of detachment from desires and emotions, to not feel totally identified and caught up in every latest whirlwind.

In the positive pole these open, animated people are involved, intensely alive, perhaps a little excitable, and full of, "Isn't life wonderful!!" enthusiasms. They are emotional and spontaneous. They go directly after what tantalizes their interest without tripping themselves worrying whether they should or shouldn't.

In the negative pole, the stimulated emotions lead to identification with feelings, an investment in how an outcome *has* to be: emotional upheavals, and, inevitably, suffering. Exasperated, "Isn't life awful!!", feelings balance out previous enthusiasms. Emotions run the gamut. Irritated, seething, overwrought, and ruffled, this pole can get pretty wearing.

Passion mode energy often does get people famous; witness all these characters who chased their enthusiasms: Joan of Arc, Martin Luther King, Jr., Pope John Paul II, Terry Cole-Whittaker, Einstein, Van Gogh, John F. Kennedy, Ralph Nader, Jane Fonda, Dustin Hoffman, Little Richard, Stevie Wonder, Frank Sinatra, Richard Ramirez and Leonard Bailey, the doctor who planted a baboon heart in Baby Faye.

Perseverance—4%
Action axis

Perseverance is as common an ingredient in success as passion. It is chosen for lifetimes when a person chooses to take on long-term tasks or karmas which must be met with determination and endurance. Perseverance makes people persistent and steady, willing to go step by step for as long as necessary to accomplish their goals. They are not the ones sporting bumper stickers proclaiming, "When the going gets tough, the tough go shopping."

In the positive pole, they are persistent, disciplined, solid, and unswerving. Garnering the discipline required for completing long term tasks is not a problem, so they usually accomplish what they set out to do despite any extenuating circumstances or hardships that might arise and be used as excuses for failure by others.

In the negative pole of perseverance, a person can appear too immutable and fixed, even a little dull. There may be a great unwillingness to change; once a goal has been set, they simply can't let go even if it becomes inappropriate, obsolete and a clear dead end. Blind to the big picture, they stay focused rather too narrowly.

Perseverance mode is handy for difficult tasks—like pulling a country together! Corazon Aquino, Khomeini, P.W. Botha, Daniel Ortega and Deng Xiaoping all use it. This mode also supports Jesse Jackson, Eddie Murphy and Robert Redford in what they choose to do.

Aggression —4%
Action mode

Aggression is another one of those English words Michael uses in a non-conventional way. From Latin into English, aggression meant attack and unprovoked offensives. With these uncomplimentary shades of meaning hovering in the background, Michael uses aggression to describe a dynamic person full of optimism and energy. Aggression mode people are vigorously energetic, especially in the use of initiative and forcefulness.

These potent people are more than willing to step in and take action; they will take more risks than most. Aggression can be an excellent way to balance a too passive previous existence, or it can be used to get a large task accomplished. Even the physical body is unusually vigorous and active when fired by aggression mode.

In the positive pole, these bold people are dynamic, adventurous, and full of life. They like action and are able to easily take stands and lead others. They are so bouncy internally that it is hard to knock them off their course. Setbacks are challenges, not traumas. Aggression mode would not dream of withdrawal.

In the negative pole, aggression turns to belligerence and assaultive, combative behaviors. Mr. or Ms. Dynamic may suddenly be full of restless energy and ready to focus it anywhere, now! Getting obnoxious seems to promise release. As power becomes brute force, this aggression can become destructive.

Examples of the numerous ways aggression mode expresses itself are found in the following people: Ronald Reagan, Moamar Khadafy, George Wallace, Nelson Mandela, Mary Kay Ash, Steven Jobs, Sean Penn, Mohammed Ali, Grace Jones, Lily Tomlin and Robin Williams.

Observation—50%
Assimilation axis

Observation is practiced by the half of our population who carefully watch and absorb what's going on around them. People using it may seem somewhat reserved and cool, for observation allows a calm, unruffled stance even in the midst of agitating circumstances. Someone "rubbernecking" in an effort to take everything in is giving off a sure clue about his mode.

Poised in the neutral position, it is the most peaceful of the modes, neither propelling a person towards action nor fanning fears. Rather it stimulates a hunger for data and is likely to cause an inquiring mind that probes and penetrates.

76

Observation mode is great for occupations from comedy to the FBI which call for investigating, analyzing, and dissecting data. Scholars like to use observation frequently because it is a proven method for learning.

When an action is called for, an observation mode person needs to slide into one of the other modes and, as usual, will have one or two favored landing spots usually chosen from passion, power, perseverance or aggression.

In the positive pole, a person gets clarity from all the watching and noticing. She will be alert, very aware and insightful, all the while maintaining observation's neutral perspective. Like a fly on the wall, she sees it all.

In the negative pole, observation may deteriorate into scrutinizing, i.e. doing exams and post mortem exams on everything—all the while withholding emotions and staying remote as a person. It is spying and surveillance instead of participation. In the negative pole, observation is more like a snake in the grass than a fly on the wall.

Julia Child, Margaret Thatcher, Paul Volcker, Anatoly Shcharansky, Rajneesh, Whoopi Goldberg, Louis Rukeyser, Dick Cavett and Barbara Walters are a few examples of people employing this mode. Observation doesn't seem to push people towards fame like aggression, power or passion modes. So despite the fact that 50% of our culture uses observation, examples were surprisingly difficult to come by.

ATTITUDES

The attitude is our most usual point of view, our most accustomed outlook on the world. It colors how we view life, how we form concepts about where we fit in, and how we go about deciding what to do or not do. Though primarily an intellectual perspective, it nevertheless immediately colors our emotions. The seven attitudes are skeptic, idealist, stoic, spiritualist, cynic, realist and pragmatist.

Motivational management experts always take into account the ultimate importance of the mind's orientation; getting and keeping a "good" attitude is crucial, they say. They remind us that our expectations, and therefore our outcomes, are ruled by our attitude. Cynics or skeptics have to downright hype themselves to get and maintain that "good" attitude these workshops tout and may become self-critical when they can't. The truth is it is much easier for an idealist or spiritualist to maintain that "good" attitude in the first place. However, Michael reminds us that we choose our overleaves for a purpose; we aren't all idealists or spiritualists every time, and that what is important is staying in the positive pole of *our* attitude, whatever it is.

Attitude is central in the Michael system too. When we remain in the positive pole of our attitude, we are more likely to be in the positive pole of the other overleaves. Atttitude is usually the first overleaf to fall into the negative side; it then drags the others. It is also the easiest overleaf for us to get our hands on and change. Keeping a "good" attitude (staying in its positive pole) is as crucial as we've been led to believe by our teachers—and mothers.

Skeptic—5%
Expression axis

Not willing to accept information at face value, skeptics are the ones who keep our systems of knowledge clean. They expect life, products, situations and intellectual theories to have a few holes in them, so they start digging to find out where the flaws are. They take network news and product breakthroughs with a grain of salt. Blind faith is never the password here.

"Oh, sure!" they say, questioning everything and usually pointing out unforseen difficulties to the rest of us. This is an intellectual frame of mind, considering this and considering that, witholding judgments until the process is complete. This attitude gives plenty of desire *and* the punch to go out and change the world.

In the positive pole, when skeptics investigate something to their satisfaction, they validate it and stand behind it 100%. Not wanting to ever be duped, they become well-informed as they strive for a very thorough form of knowledge. At best, like good scientists, they remain non-judgmental until all the data is gathered and analyzed. They strive for knowledge.

In the negative pole, uncertain and qualmish skeptics may never be satisfied in their information quests. Inconvincible and thickheaded, they remain suspicious, perhaps argumentative, and drive others away by nitpicking, making everybody's life, including their own, overly difficult.

Socrates made a virtue of skeptically questioning life to uncover and examine that which was was hidden. Other skeptics include Winnie Mandela, Louis Rukeyser, Edward R. Murrow, Jane Brody, Stephen Bingham, Herb Caen, PeeWee Herman, Woody Allen, George Burns, Katherine Hepburn and Richard Gere. In each of these people you can see in the face a minute puckering forward which subtlely lowers the brow and may cause eyes to squint slightly. That's the look of the doubter who is thinking things over.

Idealist —30%
Expressive axis

Idealists know how the world "ought to be" and exude endless enthusiasm to get it there. This attitude is so positive it gives its owner the high energy and bounce that gets others panting along to help support the vision. Buoyant idealists create lots of change in our world, though changes produced by a Baby Soul idealist like Hitler are much different from those produced by a Young Soul like John Glenn or and Old Soul like Mother Teresa.

In the positive pole, idealists fuse good ideas with reality to make things crackle. Optimistic and good-willed, they enjoy a wide sphere of influence; but when they don't get what they desire, you won't find them in a slump for long. Idealists perform the service of pulling many ideas together to make a better chair, meeting, relationship, school—or world.

In the negative pole, idealists may be immensely naive with their expectations and quite grandly disappointed when they fall through. They put people on pedestals only to experience the inevitable crushed feelings later. Idealists may become too utopian and too abstract. People complain they are annoyingly in their heads and not in reality.

Some of the many idealists who migrated into the political arena in order to change our world in as grand a directed a way as possible are John F. Kennedy, Robert F. Kennedy, John Glenn, Ronald Reagan, Martin Luther and Coretta Scott King, Imelda Marcos, Hitler, Khadafy, Clint Eastwood, Jane Fonda, and Sylvester Stallone. Others who have pursued their vision to give us a better world are Steven Jobs, Norman Cousins, Mother Teresa, Gloria Steinem, Rajneesh, Dr. Ruth Westheimer, Robert Redford, and Bruce Springsteen. A few more idealists—who can usually be recognized by the lightness in their eyes—are Linda Evans, Barbra Streisand, Lionel Richie, Eddie Murphy and Robin Williams.

Stoic —5%
Inspiration axis

This attitude is chosen for lives where a person will need the patience and forbearing it lends; for with it you pass through trying times unscathed. The attitude of stoic has been long popular in Asia in order to handle the harshness of life there. Stoicism is not usually chosen in order to influence your surroundings or change the world; the aim is to accept what is, with as much tranquility as possible. Stoics reserve their feelings—sometimes even from themselves—to avoid interference with whatever it is that life is offering.

In the positive pole, you find harmony and tranquility along with a somewhat reserved emotional nature. This enduring person enjoys stability and feels able to handle anything that develops, making the best out of situations and a virtue of necessity. Stoics may resonate with Zen, either in practice or philosophy.

In the negative pole, a stoic may be too long-suffering and dispassionate to attempt to change situations to his or her advantage. Resigned, in an unhappy way, the person remains listless about confronting problems, people, circumstances or issues. A stoic hangs in, not quitting even hopeless situations. Getting more and more exhausted, plodding along pocketing affronts, a person may become totally apathetic.

You'll recognize the stoical qualities of these seven: Joan Baez, Abraham Lincoln, Chairman Mao, George Wallace, Jean Claude Duvalier, Safia Khadafy and the baby, Meghann LaRocco, who, at less than one year old, is ready for her forth liver transplant.

Spiritualist —5%
Inspirational axis

Spiritualists have vision and a view of life that includes the unseen or the spiritual. They are wide open when looking at possibilities and well-connected to the higher planes. There is a lot of light to be found in the eyes of a spiritualist. Among Old Souls, they tend to be the ones who always remember to "white light" their cars, bless their check books and visualize their goals completed.

Being a spiritualist it is not usually something that causes a struggle; instead, it lends a very high flavor to a lifetime. These are the people who make the most of all that comes and the least of what goes.

In the positive pole, spiritualists have such a wide perspective it enables them to peer into the future to a degree. They are far-reaching and expansive, visionary, while careful to verify their beliefs and experiences. Dedicated to higher pursuits, not the mundane, spiritualists see perfection and practice perfectionism.

In the negative pole, spiritualists may be so out of touch with reality as to be nearly off the planet. Diffuse, gullible, and easily influenced, they remain ignorant of details that make the physical plane work. Taking too much on faith gets them into trouble.

Visionary Artist William Blake, *Dune's* Frank Herbert, Stevie Wonder, Michael Jackson, Liberace, Ram Dass, Rama, Swami Satchidananda, Terry Cole-Whittaker, Ralph Nader, Alice Walker and Haile Selassie are (or were) all obviously influenced by their spiritualist attitude. Syria's President Assad, a mid-Young Soul, is a spiritualist also. Since he and his country are one of the world's largest exporters of terrorism, it would be difficult to decipher just how he is using this influential overleaf without understanding the Moslem's highest deed is self-sacrifice and sacrifice of others in pursuit of the Great Cause.

Cynic — 5%
Action axis

A cynical attitude is usually taken on for protection during rugged, highly-karmic lifetimes because, by its very nature, cynicism helps fight off disappointment. Distrusting the motives of others, looking at life like it probably won't work out anyhow, and being preoccupied with the negative are trademarks of the cynic. An individual expects a certain degree of unpleasantness in life; when it comes along, a cynic is never naively suprised or suddenly overwhelmed.

In the positive pole, cynics look for what could be wrong and eliminate what is witless, unwise and too innocent. They don't take people at face value, nor advertising, nor our President. They are contradictors with a natural sense of the absurd, because they see everyone's foibles so easily. Wary and circumspect, they are not easily fooled. Cynicism may give a satiric sense of humor full of well-aimed mockery and ridicule.

In the negative pole, cynics denigrate everyone and everything... sarcastically. Caustic, full of scoffs and jeers, preoccupied with the negative "life is rotten" feeling, it becomes a tough proposition to accomplish goals, much easier to bellyache. Life in this quagmire without a bright side is no one's idea of pleasure.

People who come into positions of power or fame with the attitude of cynic have often been propelled by it. Defense Secretary Caspar Weinberger, like a little squirrel preparing for a bad winter, wants to stockpile more and more nuclear armaments and buy Star Wars, whatever the cost, because of his cynical distrust of human nature. Note in the following people that the underlying attitude of cynicism expresses itself with varying nuances: Federal Reserve Board Chairman Paul Volcker, Nicaragua's Daniel Ortega, Chile's General Pinochet, Iran's Khomeini, South Africa's P. W. Botha, John-Paul Getty, Stephen King, Whoopi Goldberg, and Richard Ramirez. Many, many mystery novelists, from Robert Parker to Evan Hunter, are cynics who create those crusty detectives suspiciously analyzing the underbelly of this culture—for our entertainment.

Realist — 30%

Realists are actually objective. Neither abstract nor speculative, they clear-headedly see what is going on without adding their own personal hopes, judgments and opinions. Fairly matter-of-fact, their comprehension of situations, along with a certain lack of sentimentality, keeps them from over-extending themselves in either personal or business life.

In the positive pole, a spade is a spade. Seeing situations as they are, without personal bias, tends to cause good judgment. Without major expectations, realists are able to be with "what is" and to stay present in the moment. Straight thinking and judicious, they see all sides to a situation and manage to accomplish a lot, even though they don't set out to change a lot.

In the negative pole, seeing all sides to an issue becomes getting lost in a muddled maze of realistic possibilities. There is an inability to choose a course of action. Objective becomes subjective, the emotions kick up, bias appears, and objective facts wiggle around annoyingly.

Here are some realists: Albert Einstein, Corazon Aquino, Henry Kissinger, Secretary of State George Shultz, Deng Xiaoping, Mae West, Madonna, Grace Jones, Joan Collins, Norman Mailer and Ernest Hemingway.

Pragmatist —20%
Assimilation axis

A pragmatist figures out what is neither feasible nor workable; he admits when a problem is insurmountable. He also easily calculates, and goes for, what is most efficient—even if it's unromantic and unlovely. A pragmatist easily eliminates impractical alternatives and then figures what "must" be done.

The neutral, assimilative axis here makes for a neutral, practical eye which reduces everything to a simple, ordered form. Like the realist, a pragmatist is neither abstract nor speculative; he is, however, more mindful of results, usefulness, advantages and disadvantages. There is usually a very shrewd common sense.

In the positive pole, the prosaic pragmatist is busy eliminating inefficiencies. These competent people are sensible, organized, and methodical. This person easily makes the rules that get a life, a relationship, an office, or a country working most efficiently.

In the negative pole, a pragmatist becomes dogmatic, which eliminates spontaneity and flexibility. Effectively blocking his growth and evolution, he allows "rules" to become God. The pragmatist then becomes rigid and narrow-minded. He may look so staid, stuffy and uninspired as to appear dull.

Famous pragmatists—who know how to get the job done—include Mary Kay Ash, Paul Newman, L. Ron Hubbard, Pope John Paul II, Prince Charles, Margaret Thatcher, Mikhail Gorbachev, Ho Chi Minh and Mexico's President Miguel de la Madrid.

CHIEF NEGATIVE FEATURES

The chief negative feature, which is an obstacle or handicap, is the only overleaf not chosen before birth. Children, particularly teenagers, experiment with all chief features—as their parents can attest—settling on one favorite usually sometime in their twenties, at least by age thirty-five.

All the chief features are based on fears. People use them for a feeling of protection in stressful times. Unfortunately, using the chief feature magnifies difficulty and magnetizes confrontation. Challenges increase. So, while the chief features may be a quick comfort, in reality they all hamper, impede, and cramp growth. Obviously this struggle creates learning experiences, but until a person gets out of the negative poles, or out of the chief feature entirely, growth toward ultimate goals is slowed.

Being aware of the chief feature allows people to know specifically how and where they tend to stumble. Do you notice yourself falling flat when you start thinking how worthless you are? When you watch the wind go out of your sails, you may, with your new recognition, decide to go easy on yourself knowing it's your habit of *self-deprecation* kicking in. As understanding grows, you don't fall into the same traps continually. As we become more tolerant of our own lapses and "handicaps", we can become more loving, or at least more tolerant, of those of others.

Chief features may be used to facilitate karmic formation and also to pay karma back. The chief feature varies from person to person in intensity and degree of use. Heavy users employ the chief feature strongly and frequently; others hardly at all. It is the one overleaf which can be erased completely from the personality. This is something many Old Souls strive to do and find possible as their lives become less and less karmic.

If you value your connections with people, you work

on your chief feature because when you fall into using it, connecting with you becomes difficult for others. It is like a wall, and when used for protection, many of the joys of intimacy and love are missed.

People who have completely erased their chief features have a very warm and caring feeling about them; nothing prickly stands in the way of their ability to love. They may also appear to be a little flat or boring to some of the rest of humanity who live off the spice and struggle provoked by the features. Examples of people, all Old Souls, with no chief features are Swami Satchidananda, Zen Master Seung Sahn, and San Francisco's Father Floyd who manages St. Anthony's Diner. Ram Dass has now nearly eliminated his chief feature of self-deprecation.

The chief feature is the only fairly flexible overleaf. That good news means that we can more easily let go of our impediments and frustrations than our goals and basic attitudes toward life.

While the features all have positive and negative poles, it is suggested that the people who have the more difficult ones of *self-destruction, self-deprecation* and *martyrdom,* aim to slide as frequently as possible to the paired features which are, in the same order, *greed, arrogance* and *impatience.* Moving out is the first step in softening or erasing the most problematic of the features.

Self-Destruction—10%
Expressive axis

People who have chosen the chief feature of self-destruction do not find life to be worth living, either because of feelings that they cannot get what they desire or are not worthy of having what they desire. Self-destruction actually tends to end a life—quickly or over the long haul. You find suicide, suicidal thoughts, daredevil behaviors, alcohol and drug abuse, terrible dietary patterns, anorexia, bulimia, prolonged illnesses, loneliness and severe depression.

To develop this chief negative feature usually requires strong imprinting from parents also bent on self-destruction. Children either model themselves on the self-destructive parents and slide right into the pattern or they resist and propel themselves right out of the familial fold.

In the positive pole, this feature may have been chosen to facilitate a karma requiring sacrifice—like risking oneself to save another. It could look like a mother pushing her child from an oncoming car by taking the brunt of the force herself. It might look like dying for a cause, a monk self-immolating, as a form of protest, or a suicide mission in the military. Thus this feature can be used as a motivation to pay back a karma which necessitates self-destruction in the process.

In the negative pole you find self-destructive habits like excessive food and alcohol, marijuana, and a whole gamut of drugs, plus beliefs like, "I don't have much to live for anyhow, so why should I stop?" The total lack of self-esteem which creates despondency and feelings of uselessness make this an unrewarding place to slog around in. It a not a pretty sight for those who care about the people doing it either.

Jim Morrison, Janis Joplin, Jimi Hendrix and more than a few other rock stars head the current list of those inclined toward self-destruction. You'll recognize the feature also in Richard Pryor and John Belushi as well as in Vincent Van Gogh and Marilyn Monroe. People who use greed heavily (see below) tend to slide into self-destructive bouts with fair frequency.

Greed—15%
Expression axis

Greed gives one heightened desires for all life has to

offer—and then creates desires for even more. A person may allow herself what she wants in great quantity but not find peace or satisfaction with it, for greed is a moving and pushy desire. It itches.

Different soul ages will respond to this chief feature in diversified ways. It may manifest as an insatiable craving for food, alcohol, sex or drugs; for money and power and fame; for more love, more relationships and more experiences; or for continual, stunning spiritual experiences. Hungers this intense tend to push people out of your life.

In the positive pole, a person in greed will ambitiously go after life and what it offers seeking fulfillment. Rarely indifferent or cool towards the physical plane, there is instead appreciation, gratitude and an allowing of abundance. Lots of energy and enthusiasm animate the person who's chasing her desires.

Voracious and insatiable in the negative pole, a person obsesses over food, drugs, love, sex, money, and power. There is an easy slide here into self-destruction. One may become ruthless in pursuit of desires. Perhaps afraid of losing what is already accumulated, a person may become selfish, hoarding, and miserly.

With the following people, you can see how the chief feature of greed can vary in the way it is used and in the desires sought: Jacqueline Kennedy Onassis, Haiti's Michele Duvalier, Henry Kissinger, Secretary of Defense Caspar Weinberger, Rajneesh, Steven Spielberg, Whoopi Goldberg, Liberace, and Mae West. California's former governor, Jerry Brown, is currently in Japan enmeshed in the study of Zen, a teaching which emphasizes dropping desire. It is his way of "growing" himself out of the heavy use of his chief feature, greed, so that he can get on with his life tasks and not be run by it.

Imelda Marcos, Robert Kennedy, Timothy Leary, Little Richard, Vicki Morgan and Mary Tyler Moore keep company as six who use greed as a chief feature *and* make (or made) strong, frequent slides into greed's more difficult paired feature, self-destruction.

Self-Deprecation—10 %
Inspiration axis

Self-deprecation is—for better or worse—the favorite chief feature of Old Souls who are dealing with self-worth issues in a universe they know to be immense. While this chief feature holds people back from forming karmas, it unfortunately also limits development by causing its users to feel of too little worth to manifest the relationships, the money, or the spiritual growth and tranquility they want. People using this feature may hold back their natural talents from manifestation.

Self-deprecation is a chief feature which has taken root in the poorer classes of many third-world countries. It is learned within the political systems which create gigantic disparities between rich and poor, making the *have-nots* believe they are not as worthwhile. While self-deprecation effectively keeps people "in their place", it tragically cuts the country off from its own energy and creativity.

Self-deprecation may look innocuous compared to self-destruction or martyrdom, but it is a feature people are encouraged to give up because it is extremely self-blocking. To loosen its hold, people need to gain a thorough understanding of their own self-worth and do some esteem building. This makes sliding into the positive pole (pride) of the paired feature (arrogance) a possibility. Making this change takes persistence over time.

In the positive pole, individuals using this feature are humble about achievements and have no need to grab acknowledgment. A great modesty exists, often due to a perspective on the universe that is unusual in our culture. In the positive pole this can be a softening overleaf; gentle, unassuming people are usually the ones using it.

In the negative pole, self-abasement, incessant apologizing and a mild to full-blown inferiority complex appear. People don't feel the self-worth to allow talents, relationships, money or spiritual growth to manifest. Self-deprecation may create a sloppy and uncaring appearance as well as lousy food and exercise habits and ultimately, poor health.

This chief feature seems to interfere with fame. The only well-known "user" to be found is Woody Allen, who's nearly made a career out of self-deprecation.

Jean-Claude Duvalier, Haiti's ex-President-for-Life, had this chief feature also. Considering that he was a Warrior using dominance and power, the chief feature helps explain his softness as well as why it was so easy for his wife and mother to run him and the country.

Arrogance—15%
Inspiration axis

Arrogance, like greed and impatience, brings notice to the person using it; plus, a person in arrogance usually centers a lot of attention on himself. This hothouse of attention on self can make for discomfort and embarrassment. Ironically, someone using this feature may shy away from attention even though he has literally spent years courting it, convincing himself and everyone in his path how superior he is. He's not sure he can stand up to all the scrutiny. Arrogance can keep a person coming and going, perpetually polishing the self-image while avoiding close contact—in case it's not yet polished enough.

Underlying arrogance is the fear of people passing unfavorable judgments on oneself. This creates the impetus to pass judgments on others first. Pasting on a princely veneer, with hopes of covering-up a (suspected) underlying unworthiness, creates barriers to intimacy.

In the positive pole, a person in arrogance will

develop pride, self-esteem and self-respect, valuing himself and his work. Arrogance tends to create an attractive, noticeable bunch of people. The role of King often favors this chief feature.

A person in the negative pole becomes so fixated on good impressions and keeping up a good show that it becomes hard to enjoy life. Vanity and snobbery pop up. Judgments of self and contempt for others create blocks to receiving life's real treats. The uncomfortable over-importance placed on self may create a ridiculously bloated character, a sort of cousin to the fillers, so rich in self-esteem, that are stuffed into your electricity and telephone bills.

Despite the push-pull feelings regarding attention tied up with arrogance, it does often help propel people to the forefront. Princess Diana and Prince Charles, Nancy and Ronald Reagan all use it as do Michael Jackson, Lionel Richie, Paul Newman, Madonna, Richard Gere, and Otto Preminger. Political Leaders with this feature are former Saudi Oil Minister Saki Yamani, France's Giscard, Mikhail Gorbachev, Ferdinand Marcos, Moamar Khadafy and Adolf Hitler. Norman Mailer, Louis Rukeyser, and Dr. Leonard Bailey use this chief feature, each with his own flair. Pope John Paul II and Swami Chidvilasananda wrestle with their arrogance, while it nearly ran Nightstalker Richard Ramirez.

Martyrdom — 15%
Action axis

Individuals with this chief feature will likely draw in more misfortune and calamity than the rest of us. However, feelings of abject misery and the tendency to blame others often drive people away from them so they don't get the sympathy they want. People with this feature feel life is out of control, and the best they can do is control others by making them feel guilty.

making them feel guilty.

Heavy users of this feature have difficulty experiencing pleasure because it interferes with their suffering. "Why don't you ever write me (call me, see me) anymore?", they want to know. Martyrs may have their crown of thorns, but they are a thorn in everyone else's side, rubbing the rest of humanity the wrong way. Others get irked; on an essence level they know being out of control is a lie, a physical plane game.

In the positive pole, a person in martyrdom is selfless, helping others without thought of his or her own personal needs. Martyrdom from this level may draw needed attention to a cause, help complete specific karmas or create a needed balance or understanding. Mother Teresa, a tireless lady who wants "to die on her feet", is an excellent example of someone staying pretty much in the positive pole of this feature.

When someone is feeling victimized and out of control in the negative pole of martyrdom, guilt tripping others for their personal wretchedness, he or she elicits disgust. The negative pole of martyrdom does not create popularity, nor even much sympathy. People stay away. Self-esteem falls below zero, a person's own needs don't get met, and the martyr, who may be slaving away, is not caring for others appropriately. Swimming in resentments and humiliations, the sour person in the negative pole creates a loathsome experience.

Thumb through a magazine or journal meant for a doctor. On those pages and pages of drug advertisements, you will see one longsuffering person after another (chief feature, martyrdom), wanly smiling with the slight relief he's gotten from the drug being touted.

Mother Teresa, Martin Luther King, Jr. and Coretta Scott King, John F. Kennedy, Beningo Aquino, Nelson Mandela, Anatoly Shcharansky, Farley Mowat and Dian Fossey all have chief features of martyrdom which they use (or used) in service to causes. Many terrorists also have martrydom as a chief feature *and* driving force in their lives.

Impatience—15%
Action axis

Impatience creates a personality ruled by time worry. Pressure, frustration and tension result from hurrying to be on to the next item on the agenda. It is difficult to be in the present when thinking about the future, and since "impatience" has a strong fear of missing out on something, it's nearly impossible to keep the mind from future-roving.

As a martyr actively tries to control people by guilt-tripping, a person in impatience tries to control time! More than good luck is obviously needed in both pursuits.

In the positive pole, impatience creates audacity and daring to relieve pressing situations. A person will plunge ahead, taking chances while moving decisively forward. When confronted by a line in the grocery store, a person in impatience will often be the first one to say, loudly, "Can't you get another checker out here?" And in the post office, again loudly, "You need to open another window!" Impatience finds creative ways to cut corners, whether it means knowing which freeway exits loop back on to the freeway to bypass some of the evening's gridlock or how to head immediately to the top of an organization in order to get a problem handled quickly.

In the negative pole, cut corners cause problems, from bungled work to angry friends and automobile accidents. When impatience kicks in strongly, a person slowed by traffic can actually feel desperate and crazy. Impatience coupled with that kind of frustration is called intolerance. Intolerance for what exists is never enjoyable; it may also cause abusive, strongly rejecting behaviors.

You can see in the personalities of the following group a tendency towards impatience which is expressed in quite dissimilar ways: Corazon Aquino, Frank Sinatra, Lily

Tomlin, Robin Williams, Katherine Hepburn and Terry Cole-Whittaker.

Stubbornness—20%
Assimilation axis

People using stubbornness can freely slide into any of the other six features. Plus they get to deal with stubbornness, which is by far the most tempting of the features to keep at a high-use level because it helps get you what you want.

In the positive pole, stubbornness lends great determination, which can be an important element in anybody's success. Stubborn people will have the resolve and the ability to pierce through barriers and bottlenecks. It has to do with self-possession, knowing you have the power to get what you want. Stubbornness gives backbone, diligence and perseverance.

In the negative pole, there is obstinacy: mulish, headstrong, stiffnecked, inflexible people pushing to get their own way. When stubborness misfires, its users are basically unable to listen to others, especially to suggestions or advice. "I'll do it my way, myself." Tenacious and dogged become obdurate and stuck. Stonewall solid, these people put on the brakes even when it is quite detrimental to themselves. There is a great fear of change here, so much so that growth can grind to a halt.

Examples of behavior from the chief feature stubbornness can be found in Chairman Mao, South Africa's P. W. Botha, Panama's General Noriega, Japan's Prime Minister Nakasone, Secretary of State George Shultz, George Wallace, Grace Jones, Barbra Streisand, Simone de Beauvoir, Stephen King, Georgia O'Keefe, Steven Jobs, and Billy Graham.

CHAPTER SIX
CENTERING

Although there are seven centers, which roughly correspond to the seven main chakras, the vast majority of people actively operate out of the main three—**emotional, moving** or **intellectual centers.**

When you respond immediately to something, you do so with your favored centering. An intellectually centered individual might respond to the loss of a job with analysis, reasons, and lots of cogitation, while an emotionally centered person would respond with feelings—hurt, anger, sadness, etc. A moving centered person would likely respond with movement and action, perhaps by immediately going out to look for another job, going to play racquetball, or by being uncomfortably restless and fidgety. Each of these three main centerings is chosen equally on a worldwide basis; our culture is interestingly biased—50% choose intellectual centering, 40% choose emotional centering, and a small 10% choose moving or kinesthetic centering.

The intuitive, emotionally centered individual processes incoming data from life more quickly than anyone; feeling works fast, compared to the slower process of pushing something through the intellect. Emotional centering gives a deep sense of knowing, the ability to respond sympathetically and get to the heart's core of issues. It may create mawkishness also, or hysteria. Mature souls favor this centering because of the intensity it lends to relationships.

Each person has one primary center he or she uses *and* a part of one other center which is used as a backup. Thus an emotionally centered woman may use intellectual center secondarily, flipping back and forth between feeling and thinking; or she may use the moving center secondarily and be concerned with doing something with her feelings and emotions, perhaps by becoming a singer, an actor, a dancer, a preacher, or a healer.

Public figures who move with their feelings (i.e. use the moving part of emotional center) are Martin Luther King, Jr., Nancy Reagan, Lily Tomlin, Stevie Wonder, Linda Evans and Madonna. While these people have made a splash with their lives, choosing centering which does not include the intellectual can make for a difficult time growing up in America. We are a mental culture; our schools are training grounds for the intellect. A child without easy access to at least a part of intellectual center will likely, to the despair of parents, feel uninterested in academic school life—oftentimes to the detriment of the child's own self-esteem.

The intellectual part of basic emotional centering is used by Stephen Spielberg, Woody Allen, Lionel Richie, Ronald Reagan, Deng Xiaoping and Coretta Scott King. Spielberg has a genius for stirring emotion, as well as satisfying it, with his movies. Were he primarily intellectually centered, his movies wouldn't cast such spells.

Moving centered people—a wee 10% of our culture—tend to be constant balls of activity, restless and on the move. These people are often attracted to sports, aviation, race cars, police work, construction, painting, camp counseling, raft trip navigating, outside sales work, and anything else that keeps them moving. They may pace, fidget, and move from one activity to the next without completing what they've promised everyone, including themselves, to complete.

Nikita Khrushchev banging his shoe on the UN's lectern is in a perfect moving-center fury of action, as are PeeWee Herman and Bette Midler most of the time.

When using the emotional center as the secondary centering, moving center individuals would be familiar with their emotional natures, perhaps to use that to fuel movement—as in dance. With input from a secondary intellectual centering, movement would be directed with great intention and forethought.

Sylvester Stallone, who's films are famous for action with emotional content, is a Warrior using the emotional part of moving center. Sage Eddie Murphy, who also uses that combination, is a very much more talkative example of the same centering. Artisan Sean Penn, who displays a tendency to punch photographers, is also moving-centered with emotional center input. Penn's impulses towards "movement" filter through his young age and hormones right into the negative poles of his dominance goal and aggression mode. Mae West and Tina Turner are two women who use(d) this centering.

Princess Diana, obviously a very bright young woman, has been quoted saying her brain is "...the size of a pea," and, when challenged to Trivial Pursuit, "...as thick as a plank." She an example of a moving-centered person, who loves to dance, play and be active, with a secondary (warmhearted) emotional centering. That her intellect is not her strong suit obviously causes her some distress. In our mental society, moving center, without a secondary intellectual centering, can create the sense of being a misfit and a subsequent downturn in self-esteem—even though the person has plenty of intelligence, understanding, and wits.

A person without any moving centering will be less inclined to give the body the exercise it requires; another downside may be a tendency to *do* little, for the impulse is to think and feel but not to grab the results to go do something. However, the impetus towards *doing* is also be enhanced by overleaves from the rest of the action axis, especially dominance, submission, aggression, perseverance and impatience—or by being a Warrior or a King.

Paul Newman, who often zooms through his movies in some way or another, is moving centered with secondary intellectual centering. Robin Williams, Whoopi Goldberg, Fred Astaire, Dr. Ruth Westheimer, author Ken Kesey and Mother Teresa also exemplify that centering. Stephen Bingham, an activist (and moving-centered) California lawyer, when accused of helping a Black Panther escape from prison, left California, moved around, then moved to Paris where he became a house-painter, only to re-surface years later in California in order to clear his name. How's that for a moving-centered life?

Intellectual centering creates the braininess and left-brained manner of thinking so highly valued in our culture; it may give a scintillating, sparkling, and discriminating mind. The nimble-minded kids who succeed most easily in school (it interests them) and on I.Q. tests usually have this centering. While intellectual center is primarily linear in function, there is plenty of room for clear thought and insight; intellectual center alone may not give thoughtfulness, common sense or wisdom, qualities which are more associated with the emotional center.

An intellectually centered person using moving center secondarily will not "get" emotions too easily; on the other hand, he or she will be inclined to take ideas and put them out into the world. John Kennedy, Pat Robertson, Syria's Hafez Assad, Henry Kissinger, Orson Welles, Frank Herbert *(Dune)*, Gloria Steinem and Rajneesh are all intellectually centered with easy access to their moving center. All are the type to take an idea and move it into popular culture for as great an effect as possible.

An intellectually centered individual who's secondarily using emotional center will dart back and forth between thinking and feeling, each fueling the other—for better or worse. Katherine Hepburn, Dustin Hoffman, Mary Tyler Moore, Margaret Thatcher, Richard Nixon, Tip O'Neill, Peter Jennings, Barbara Walters and Timothy Leary illustrate this way of centering.

While the **instinctive** center is a place some people spend their lifetime, it is also a place we all enter daily while attending to toilet activities, showering, or perhaps while jogging, doing tai chi, folding the laundry, weeding the flower garden or plugging in the two-hundreth call on Macy's switchboard. One lands in instinctive center through calming, repetitive activities. The instinctive center *can* then be used as a doorway to higher states of consciousness.

The instinctive center has access to information about both current environmental conditions and past life memories. It does not function according to linear time; all time is <u>now</u> to the instinctive center. Because its primary function is to insure the survival of the body, there are a lot of "Watch Out For That!!" messages packed into it, whether relevant to the current life or not.

When people spend a whole lifetime in the instinctive center—which happens more in Infant and Baby Soul times—there starts to be a paranoia that develops from living in the midst of those all too blatant "Watch Out!!" messages.

LSD created vivid, visual, instinctive center tours for many, sometimes with healing, broadening effects and sometimes with lifelong, not-so-happy side effects.

Criminals who have that crazed look in their eyes (like Charles Manson or Richard Ramirez) are often spending most of their time in the instinctive center, as are many institutionalized people. Hitler lived primarily out of instinctive center, as does Libya's Khadafy, who, as a for instance, hasn't slept in the same location for more than one or two or nights in a row in years. The men who shot Pope John Paul II and Indira Ghandi are both doing instinctive center lifetimes—behind bars at this point.

Stephen King, a Sage and author of hair-raising horror stories, is an early Baby Soul hanging out in late Infant Soul consciousness *and* his own raw instinctive center. His stories make use of the primal instinctive issues to which he has such easy access. Both the skittish PeeWee Herman and comedian Bob Goldthwait, who's onstage sputtering misfit of a character is either on the verge of a nervous breakdown or marginally recovered, use their creative energies to bring up fearful, instinctual stuff for the rest of us. Under the guise of entertainment, these three individuals allow audiences to touch into the same kind of scared, panicky places in their own psyches, and thus create an opportunity to stop repressing and start integrating.

A person can use instinctive center to let go of an old pattern and change the direction of her life. Becoming very ill or experiencing a high fever or lots of pain shuts down moving, intellectual and even emotional centers, driving a person into instinctive center, thus allowing time for an extensive, always more or less unconscious, review.

The last three centers are the higher centers—**higher intellectual, higher emotional** and **higher moving** centers. Though these centers give a feeling of enlightenment when a person is using them, they are not something we choose before birth but rather a way we learn to be through meditation, prayer and other spiritual practices.

In higher intellectual center, the intellect is in touch with spiritual realms and the deeper truths of existence. *Healing Our World, Beyond War* and various other peace organizations are examples of groups based on principles right out of the higher intellectual center. These groups aim to get the world in touch with the truths experienced here. Intellectual types most frequently get into the higher intellectual center space; many, many people touch in here from time to time during a day. Nicholas Danilof, the American journalist whose jailing in the Soviet Union caused such an uproar, is an example of a person with frequent access to this center where the mind feels whole and in touch with the whole.

In the higher emotional center, a person is in touch with the highest of feelings; a kind of universal love and a heartfelt compassion come beaming through. This often comes with meditation and has a spillover effect into life. The drug called Ecstasy or ADM, now illegal, had the ability to create these higher emotional states of overwhelming joy and rapture. People who have seen the pleasure of this kind of harmonious state often strive to keep it in their lives. Of course, the point is to create these kinds of states for ourselves with love, not with drugs.

Higher moving center has a very kinesthetic feel, which may sometimes be experienced while making love. A person who can do hands-on, physical healing is often using the higher moving center because it does give the ability to transform matter with its use. The waving-armed, up-and-down-on-his-toes, kind of preacher is often whipping up the energy of an audience via the higher kinesthetic center. It is very charismatic.

CHAPTER SEVEN
FREQUENCY
MALE/FEMALE ENERGY

FREQUENCY

Along with the role, what else *doesn't* change from life to life is a person's frequency and the ratio of male to female energy exhibited.

Frequency is how fast or slow a person vibrates or hums, how he or she resonates with this planet. Frequency is actually felt out and chosen by the individual essences in the cadre before role, essence twin or much of anything else is decided upon.

One essence will be aware it enjoys being with the quickness of a butterfly or a lightening bolt, while another will appreciate the stillness of a lake or mountain of rock. The essences who will become solid roles like Warrior, King and Scholar tend to prefer the lower frequencies. Those who become the most fluid roles, Artisan and Priest, will usually enjoy the the higher frequencies. Servers will tend to prefer the low middle range, while Sages are found high, low and in the middle. Life is intricate and complex; no role is ever *always* high or *always* low.

Michael measures frequency for humans on a scale

Michael measures frequency for humans on a scale from one to one hundred. A mountain or rock has an exceedingly low frequency, much slower than a person with the exceedingly low frequency of one, while a hummingbird's frequency is much higher and buzzier than a person displaying the highest human frequency of one hundred. Golda Meier, a Warrior, had a much more solid feel—and lower frequency—than Priest Nancy Reagan.

A Priest with a relatively slow (for Priests) frequency of 40 looks far more grounded and stable than a Priest buzzing around with a frequency of 90. People with higher frequencies often feel held back by the solidity of the earth plane and greatly enjoy, between lives (and in altered states and dreams), the freedom and quickness of the astral plane. They are the ones who easily fly around in meditation but have difficulty staying in their bodies for day-to-day life.

Those with lower frequencies have a great love and affection for the physical plane, relishing the pleasures here and the "reality" of it all. These people don't partake of such long astral "vacations" between lives and tend to be the ones using many more lives to get through each soul age.

MALE/FEMALE ENERGY

Each individual also takes on a particular ratio of male to female energy for the cycle of lifetimes. The ratio has nothing to do with male or female bodies, though it may have to do with a preference for being one sex over the other.

Male energy is a highly focused type of energy which puts a defined pinpoint of light on what it is surveying, looking at one thing at a time in an orderly fashion. It is grounded, productive, and to the point.

Female energy is bubblier, more creative and chaotic. It is not focused, but rather very broad in its view. A female-energy person will be full of "good ideas" almost continually and may not bother with an organized follow-through, because generating ideas is fun and easy, while focus can be like pulling teeth. He or she will appear to have an enormous, fluffy essence or aura and will tend to dress more softly than the tailored, male energy types.

A person with strong male energy will be focused on the details of how to get things done but typically can't step outside those details to view the broad, and perhaps changing, perspective. Quite different in scope of vision, these types can balance and help each other when not making each other wrong.

Albert Einstein, who often could not find his way home from the lab, is an example of an intensely female-energied person. Woody Allen is aware of his large "feminine component". Most of our TV journalists, Ted Koppel being one obvious example, have hardheaded male-energy minds.

Many people display frequencies of around 50, and a 50/50 balance of male to female energy. Others, not wanting one second of boredom, opt for the extremes in both, sensing it will be an interesting and exciting thing to take on. It is, and troublesome too.

CHAPTER EIGHT
IMPRINTING

Cultural conditioning to behave in a certain way is something we all pick up with our birth packet. We receive a particular mother, a father (present or absent), relatives, neighbors and schools, all in a certain side of town and part of the country, working together to tell a child, "This is what life is about, and this is how one acts." Parents especially influence their children's intellectual and moral development. For instance, a parent's competence in solving the dilemmas of daily life helps shape a child's problem-solving abilities, as does something so simple as a parent's propensity for early rising or ritual flossing.

Many adult habit patterns and characteristics come directly from imitating parents—whether it be walking, talking, speaking, thinking habits or values themselves. When shouting at a child, many have had the experience of feeling it is their own mother's or father's voice coming out of their own mouths; and when a child grows and shouts back, it is often in your voice and your words.

Michael calls this early conditioning *imprinting*. Most of it happens by age seven, and all of it is complete by fourteen. Imprinting is in-service training which grooms you to get going and handle life. Since it can also be like the blind leading the blind, there comes a point when it is mandatory to drop indoctrination to gain your own adult viewpoint and flexibility.

Children are not born as "blank slates" ready for their parents to mold them towards crime and violence, fame and success, or spiritual enlightenment. Babies have personalities they will develop based on the overleaves they've chosen before birth, as well as past life influences and karma to deal with.

In our culture, everyone receives a strong dose of Young Soul imprinting. This impetus to master the physical plane can be very helpful; its downside is that Old Souls often feel something is wrong—with themselves.

While they know they're as smart and as deserving as the next guy, it seems hard to pull their (physical plane) lives together. The strength of Young Soul cultural imprinting is so huge, it's difficult, even for a self-reflective Old Soul, to understand his or her own lack of ambition. Once on the material plane, a personality always desires material things. However, for Old Souls, the push the essence gives will not be towards worldly acquisition but rather towards spiritual and philosophical growth.

Infant Souls, who are two steps in the other direction from Young, don't relate well to Young Soul imprinting and usually avoid it by staying in simpler cultures where they get less of it. With all the basic trust and survival issues that need to be handled, Infant Souls find our capitalistic culture with it's loose family structure, entrepreneurship, tax forms, checking accounts and monthly bills, due now, needlessly complicated and threatening.

Another kind of imprinting is *role* imprinting. This is where parents impress their children with the virtue and rightness of their own role(s) as a way of acting and perceiving the world. For instance, a Sage child in a family with Server and Warrior parents will not get much reinforcement to be expressive, whether it's discussing feelings, standing out in a group, mouthing-off, or simply acting funny.

Rather, this Sage will receive imprinting on how people should be helpful, hard working, organized and probably quiet—which is exactly what the child "hired" the parents to do. Imprinting can be very helpful, or it can be like chains that need to be thrown off in later life. In that case, the struggle is part of the reason the child chose the parents.

Imprinting always causes a reaction, but people respond in different ways. Some may rebel and fight against strong imprinting, while others agree with it and take it on, more or less consciously, as their own. Much imprinting is so powerful people don't even know it exists, which allows it to exert a pervasive, subtle influence on belief systems. Everyone chooses all imprinting for the boost it gives to growth, even though the boost may only look like a decades-long battle to shed it.

Once you have figured out your role or had that information channeled, take notice of whether you are actually doing, expressing or feeling the kinds of things your role likes. Often imprinting from parents or society frustrates the easy expression of your role. Examples abound: a boy pushing himself into athletics where, if his true self could arise, he might prefer library time; a girl, imprinted by Artisans, who struggles to become a designer, but would probably prefer to be a "less creative" doctor or nurse; a boy, imprinted by Warriors, who loves to dance and perform, but pursues a legal career; and that proverbially meek woman who's actually a powerhouse underneath the pliant mask she learned to wear.

CHAPTER NINE
ESSENCE TWINS AND
TASK COMPANIONS

ESSENCE TWINS

This is a term Michael uses to refer to a pairing of individual essences which occurs before any part of the entity has started to incarnate onto this planet. An essence twin becomes the most intimate continuing relationship experienced during the cycle of earthly lives. Also the most challenging.

The two essences are complementary halves on the essence level, an internal mirror image of each other. Tear a piece of paper down the middle; like essence twins, the two halves may not look much like each other, but they do make a perfect fit. Your essence twin knows who you are, deep down, and overall is very supportive. But here comes the paradox. Since you mirror each other, essence twins challenge, provoke, spin each other around, and very infrequently let each other off the hook. No one can get inside you so well. These are not stable, predictable relationships but intense, engaging, and usually fascinating.

Despite the wealth of similar experience built up over

many lifetimes and the intimate sharing between lives on the astral plane, essence twins are usually more different than alike, usually in personality as well as essence. Essence twin pairings are usually chosen to give more breadth to the pair. Generally speaking, that means different roles. Most often they choose to balance each other with male/female energy and with frequency too. If one essence is a very low frequency, focused male-energy type, it's quite likely the chosen "twin" will be a buzzy, bubbly, creative female-energy type. It will be a case of opposites attracting, often driving each other crazy, and always provoking lots of growth.

If one essence has a mid-range frequency and a 50/50 balance of male/female energy, the essence twin will also usually be found in the middle ranges. The relationship will be easier to handle that way, but looks less interesting from the astral point of view, because there's less experimental push-pull. Souls who have been through many complete cycles on other planets are the ones most fascinated by the difficult-to-handle extremes.

Because Infant, Baby and Young Souls generally feel some fear about closeness, and because fears of intimacy amplify prodigiously within sexual relationships, essence twins are not often lovers in those earlier phases. Instead they parent one another; they become siblings, cousins, special aunties; or they become close, sometimes inseparable, friends, co-workers—or enemies. In this way, over many lifetimes, knowledge of each other grows, and trust develops so that by the Mature and Old cycles essence twins are prepared for the true deep intimacy that may develop.

Essence twins know each other so well and so often that each will have a great deal of bleed-through showing up from the other's role. Bleed-through gives each partner extra oomph. A Sage with a Scholar essence twin will look more stable and grounded than a Sage with zingy Priest bleed-through, while a Sage with an Artisan essence twin, like Carmen Miranda, is likely to be exalted in a zany, doubly expressive, kind of way. This blending is particularly obvious in couples who've been together for decades.

A very strong intermingling of energies or roles also comes about when only one essence twin is on the planet. The astral partner will usually beam sizable amounts of energy toward the land-bound essence twin. Werner Erhard, a sixth level Old Sage, is an example of this. The energy of his cycled-off essence twin, a King, makes Erhard more exalted in looks and appeal. The Sage makes for excellent expression and communication; the King bleed-through gives power and the impetus towards mastery.

Because the Mature period explores emotionality and intimate connections, essence twins come together then frequently as sexual partners. Liz Taylor and Richard Burton are a vivid example of that Mature Soul brand of essence twin emotional volatility, the clincher being "Can't live with 'em, and can't live without 'em." Madonna and Sean Penn may step in to take their place as the next famous pair of essence twins bent on pushing each other to extremes.

Jean-Paul Sartre (Artisan) and Simone de Beauvoir (Warrior) are a pair of Mature essence twins who maintained an intense, lifelong relationship. They chose not to live together and thought themselves wise. It is likely that their valued, thought-out rational behavior would have been more difficult to maintain sharing bed, bath, cooking and four or five rooms.

"Two Souls with but a single thought; two hearts that beat as one. . ." This seems to have more to do with romance novels than your average essence twin relationship. While essence twins are our soul mates on one level, and we really do know them better than anyone, it is only rarely that they manifest as that longed for, peaceful, romantically blessed relationship. Essence twins seem to take care *not* to be the perfect, always kind, prince and princess who never have their own concerns or agendas to worry about. Even in the Old Soul period, the essence twin relationship is an intense, not easy to handle involvement —which is sought after vigorously.

Michael does not use the term "soul mate" because it brings some false concepts into play. There is no person who is a better mate for you in every lifetime nor one with whom you have mated consistently down through the centuries; imagine how limited growth would be if that were the case. You may in fact hang out with a handful of people in a high proportion of lifetimes and be teachers, students, parents, siblings, jailors, rescuers, slanderers, healers, deserters, attackers, patrons, masters and slaves for each other. Michael calls these monads or monadal relationships; they are a common way to gather information, deepen experience of another being, and to grow. When you set it up to be a lover or a mate with one of these people, it is likely there will be immediate mutual attraction which feels like it goes back forever. And it does, but not because you are always mated. You both knew each other well in extremely diverse and challenging situations which have been balanced over time, so there is no charge left, simply fondness.

When essence twins meet and bond and blend with each other, it helps the rest of their lives to flow more easily. It is an ultimate kind of lesson in agape to accept your essence twin and give her the room to be truly who she is.

It is also a difficult task on many levels; the intimacy levels are tough. Essence twins are so connected they think they "own" each other and will typically act in ways they never would with other humans. Old Souls, in particular, like to set up their essence twin relationships to be real challenges. A young Southern woman, falling for a black man (or woman) or the urge to mate despite a 20 to 30 year age and imprinting gap would not be atypical Old Soul "good ideas". With an essence twin there is a need to have lots of communication and clarity—which is hard to initiate, much less keep going, because of the continual intensity.

To allow a separate identity for your essence twin, you must be strong and centered yourself. The idea is to get to acceptance no matter how difficult your essence twin is; then you will be powerfully linked. You may get your essence twin out of your romantic life, but you don't get her out of your mind without creating a comfortable connectedness first; the whole essence twin issue will gnaw at you until it's handled. Considering how difficult these couplings are, it is actually surprising that essence twins manage to mate in one-third of their lifetimes overall.

Usually people do not choose to meet essence twins until their late twenties or thirties. This gives each an opportunity to do their karmas with other people and avoids some of the obsessions that get stirred up if the couple meets too early. The Duke and Duchess of Windsor are an example of a couple meeting after they had done most of their karmas. Since part of her karma was to marry and divorce, he had to leave the British throne to be with her. Princess Diana met her essence twin quite early, though Prince Charles's timing was right on the button.

Here's some more essence twin couples: Jane Fonda and Tom Hayden; Sam Shepard and Jessica Lange; Harry and Bess Truman; Imelda and Ferdinand Marcos; Michele and Jean-Claude Duvalier; Mikhail Gorbachev and wife Raisa Gorbachev. Ronald Reagan's essence twin was first wife, Jane Wyman. He and Nancy have a comfortable husband and wife monad.

When an essence twin relationship is between parent and child, there are some patterns which frequently pop up. Families with essence twins are often, but by no means always, the ones where parent/child incest gets set off. Or these may be the families where the child never moves out, or where the adult child moves his new wife into the family home seeing no reason to leave essence twin Mom. Often these situations with adult familial essence twins under one roof work out quite well.

Hugh Hefner, a Sage not too well set up for trust and intimacy with women this lifetime, is essence twins with his Warrior daughter, Christie Hefner, whom he does trust to run the family business.

Parents will sometimes both have an essence twin among the children. This works out relatively well by helping to avoid the jealously evoked by the intensity of an essence twin relationship that only one parent enjoys. The left-out parent, sensing the closeness between the essence twins, may take a strong disliking and competitive stance towards the child.

After a lifetime together, it is enormously painful to remain on the physical plane after your essence twin has died. Buckminster Fuller died just hours after his wife—and essence twin. He had not yet been informed of her death. Essence twins Roy Rogers and Dale Evans found it so difficult to let Trigger go that they stuffed him. It's nearly assured that that this pair will choose to pass on very close in time to each other—as do millions of other essence twin couples every year.

TASK COMPANIONS

The relationship task companions create is altogether easier. Essence twins are related internally, with each pressing the other towards growth. Task companions are related externally, each supporting the other with tasks that are usually of an enduring sort.

Like essence twins, this pairing is chosen before starting the cycle on this planet. Task companions will usually find each other compatible partners, almost like two oxen under the same yoke, for the agendas they've set up to complete. Much can be accomplished with these good working relationships.

The tasks the pair will work on are usually quite long-term and may be occupational or non-occupational. Building one partner's self-confidence (or self-control) could become one lifelong mission. Sometimes task companions help each other handle being their least favorite sex. For instance, a person who adores being a woman will have the task companion's support in figuring out how to pull of being male without feeling miserably scrunched.

A task often has to do with developing a talent, which could range from the ability to sell, to the ability to excel in music, to the ability to be psychic. Having the easy, calm, compatible, loving support of a task companion who wants to help you obviously boosts the ability to acquire a talent.

Task companions who do become husband and wife will compatibly settle into a pleasant marriage. The task could be to raise a large family, open a business together or set an example of male/female communication for others to experience.

Like an essence twin, a task companion usually shows up later in life when both are ready to do the tasks. Just by meeting they remind each other of agreements made before birth and thus bring clarity to each other's lives. Meeting too early can bring on frustration because the pair will likely be wanting, even striving, to do tasks that are not yet ripe.

Many mentor situations in business, where an older person helps a younger one learn the ropes, are task companions at work. Brooke Shields, an Artisan, and her powerful backstage Server mother, Terry, are task companions. The mother managed to push, and keep, the daughter in the limelight, orchestrating career, publicity and now an education with little resentment on the daughter's part.

Prince Andrew, a Sage, and Sarah Ferguson, a Server, are task companions settling into what will likely be a compatible marriage—despite what the gossipy newspapers have to say. Woody Allen and Mia Farrow have a task companion relationship; they inspire each other and work easily together.

"Good night, Chet."

"Good night, David."

Remember those nightly sign-offs? This was the task companion news team of Chet Huntly and David Brinkly.

CHAPTER TEN
CREATING PERSONALITY

Each lifetime we decide on a growth-plan, grab our handful of overleaves, a couple of parents, a body, and we're off and running. This chapter takes a deeper look at what is actually created with that handful of overleaves.

Some lifetimes we choose overleaves that are all essentially on "go-mode," i.e. there is no element in the created personality that is likely to constrict or hold us back, and the overleaves don't tangle with each other to cause discomfort.

Below are some full sets of overleaves for people with goals of dominance who have chosen to make a splash this lifetime.

This woman is truly a powerhouse; her chief feature sometimes leads her around, but doesn't trip her too often.

Madonna
King/Artisan essence twin
Dominance—goal
Power—mode
Realist—attitude
Arrogance—chief feature
Emotional Center/Moving Part
Mature, 4/5 level

With the next person, another competent King, there is a sense of being more intricately wired, more thoughtful and not quite *such* a force of nature. The chief feature seems to provoke temper here; it is rather mildly under control.

Katharine Hepburn
King/Artisan essence twin
Dominance—goal
Passion—mode
Idealist—attitude
Impatience—chief feature
Intellectual Center/Moving Part
Mature, 6/7 level

Contrast the overleaves of the following person with those of Katharine Hepburn. They have goal, mode and attitude in common, and both are solid, action roles with expressive essence twin influences. While one can see traces of the same kind of personality strands in both, they are extremely different people. The soul age, which always makes for very different life tasks, creates a big difference here, as does the centering.

Sylvester Stallone
Warrior/Sage essence twin
Dominance—goal
Passion—mode
Idealist—attitude
Arrogance—chief feature
Moving Center/Emotional Part
Young, fourth level

Here's another interesting character who obviously functions quite smoothly out of her set of overleaves. Aggression mode and moving center both make her very good with physical roles; stubbornness makes her feel all the more extraordinarily solid.

Grace Jones
Warrior/Artisan essence twin
Dominance—goal
Aggression—mode
Realist—attitude
Stubborness—chief feature
Moving Center/Emotional Part
Young, fifth level

This next person is better known by accomplishments than by personality. His overleaves do hint at why he was able to accumulate so much wealth and to keep going after more without second thoughts. Cynicism, which holds many back, seems to have been used here as one more reason to push forward. Sixth level lives tend to be very karmic, and the Young Soul stage will be creating karma as well as paying it off.

John-Paul Getty
King/Priest essence twin
Dominance—goal
Power—mode
Cynic—attitude
Greed—chief feature
Moving Center/Intellectual Part
Young, sixth level

This person has strong overleaves, and at fourth level young is ready to be out in the world, but got tripped up by heavy use of her chief feature—which hasn't calmed down all that much even recently. When greed gets going strong, it transforms itself all too often into self-destruction. A Priest, who's further inspired by her centering and attitude, she remains connected in feeling, with a much professed love, to "her people".

Imelda Marcos
Priest/Warrior essence twin
Dominance—goal
Power—mode
Idealist—attitude
Greed—chief feature
Emotional Center/Moving Part
Young, fourth level

This next person handles his chief feature, also greed, with a little more grace. As a Mature soul, he's had more experience with it.

Henry Kissinger
Warrior/Sage essence twin
Dominance—goal
Passion—mode
Realist—attitude
Greed—chief feature
Intellectual Center/Moving Part
Mature, fourth level

The next person, also a political player, has a more complicated world role—and more complicating overleaves. Here's a quote that shows up the dominance, the perseverance and the cynicism: "Killing is mercy, for it seeks to rectify the person. A person sometimes cannot be rectified unless he is cut up and heated up. You must kill, burn and lock up those who are in opposition."

Ayatollah Khomeini
Warrior/Priest essence twin
Dominance—goal
Perseverance—mode
Cynic—attitude
Arrogance—chief feature
Moving Center/Intellectual Part
Baby, acting also out of Infant

This person has also obtained an influential world position with a somewhat similar, though softer, set of overleaves. His personality could be fighting with itself; instead its parts are uniquely parceled out. With submission, he's become devoted to communist ideals; with cynicism, very anti-American; and with perseverance, he is not going to be moved easily out of our way.

Daniel Ortega
Scholar/Warrior essence twin
Submission—goal
Perseverance—mode
Cynic—attitude
Arrogance—chief feature
Intellectual Center/Emotional Part
Baby, seventh level

Below are two more people with submission as a goal, both with the uncomplicated overleaves that help to push them—and their principles—into the limelight. Passion mode makes them both excited about causes and gives the impetus for going after whatever it is that grabs them. Remember that arrogance doesn't necessarily put someone's nose in the air, but may get a person wrestling with issues regarding his own self-worth, even to the point of ducking attention and publicity.

Pope John Paul II
Warrior/Scholar essence twin
Submission—goal
Passion—mode
Pragmatist—attitude
Arrogance—chief feature
Emotional Center/Moving Part
Mature, fourth level, Baby sometimes

Ralph Nader
Warrior/ Priest essence twin
Submission—goal
Passion—mode
Spiritualist—attitude
Arrogance—chief feature
Intellectual Center/Moving Part
Mature, third level

The following person now heads the only country in the world with the word "love" in its constitution. That viewpoint is a result of her soul age, emotional centering and her ability to stay in the positive pole of her goal so much of the time. Perseverance has not only helped her persist through incredibly difficult times, but it helps keep a mild chief feature in check.

Corazon Aquino
Sage/Warrior essence twin
Acceptance—goal
Perseverance—mode
Realist—attitude
Impatience—chief feature
Emotional Center/Intellectual Part
Mature, seventh level

Our President has similar overleaves, but with an interesting little tangle between his goal of acceptance and aggression mode. Acceptance makes him Mr. Nice Guy, wanting to ingratiate so people like him, while aggression—which also helps him be so bouncy—often causes him to vigorously pursue something regardless of the feelings, desires or reactions of others. This creates some complication within his personality and is one reason it is difficult for him to be totally straightforward.

Ronald Reagan
Sage/Warrior essence twin
Acceptance—goal
Aggression—mode
Idealist—attitude
Arrogance—chief feature
Emotional Center/Intellectual Part
Mature, second level

Here's a person having a lot of fun with an easy set of overleaves in a lifetime with the major physical disability of blindness.

Stevie Wonder
Priest/Server essence twin
Acceptance—goal
Passion—mode
Spiritualist—attitude
Arrogance—chief feature
Emotional Center/Moving Part
Old, second level

When people choose overleaves that are difficult, like caution mode cynic with a goal of discrimination, usually there is a self-karma playing itself out. A person with these overleaves would not easily push herself into public consciousness, or even into any consciousness that was very pleasant, but would likely spend much of her time wrestling with her observations. Passion mode or power mode would not lighten the situation much, though she'd likely become noticed more quickly, for better or worse.

Caution mode mixed with idealism would tend to grate internally creating confusion and distress. In the same way, a goal of acceptance mixed with a skeptical or cynical attitude would plunge one into difficulties from the get-go.

The point here is that many people end up with overleaves that put them at cross-purposes, creating one internal predicament after another. While that kind of discomfort may create growth, it does not tend to create much outward momentum, much less fame. Nevertheless, what follows are a few well-known people with unwieldy thickets of overleaves.

The person below has chosen a such difficult bunch of overleaves that they seem to turn him inside out at times. He tends to be reclusive, and you don't get the idea it is a necessarily joyful experience. Discrimination is rarely easy, but imagine also being a skeptic with passion mode impulses—push-pull, push-pull, push-pull.

Bob Dylan
Priest/Warrior essence twin
Discrimination—goal
Passion—mode
Skeptic—attitude
Greed—chief feature
Moving Center/Intellectual Part
Mature, 2/3 level

Here's a quote from *Time* about the head of "The Talking Heads", "David's a paradox. He's the most absent-present person I've ever met." He is also stunningly creative. Moving center has him hopping around during concerts while repression mode puts him in funny little suits and adds a strange refinement to the hopping.

David Byrne
Scholar/Artisan essence twin
Discrimination—goal
Repression—mode
Cynic—attitude
Arrogance—chief feature
Moving Center/Intellectual Part
Early Mature, often manifesting Young

Next, a very favorite person in America. Acceptance, along with his overused, noisy chief feature of self-deprecation, makes him endearing, while his passion mode skeptic landed him in analysis for a famously long time. Notice how his overleaves play against each other.

Woody Allen
Artisan/Scholar essence twin
Acceptance—goal
Passion—mode
Skeptic—attitude
Self-deprecation—chief feature
Emotional Center/Intellectual Part
Mature, fifth level

And finally, a look at two people who chose to do heavy investigations of their instinctive centers this lifetime. One of them handles it very well, creating a lucrative career out of material straight from this center. He has allowed many people to look at the similar stuff they carry in their own instinctive centers, let it be chilling and scary, and then let it dissipate. The Sage gives the storytelling ability and the King essence twin lends an ability to master it at a very early soul age. Considering this set of rather somber overleaves, this individual is doing fabulously well in life.

Stephen King
Sage/King essence twin
Re-evaluation—goal
Caution—mode
Cynic—attitude
Stubborn—chief feature
Instinctive Center/Intellectual Part
Baby, often manifesting Infant

Here we have a Server with a Server essence twin. Imagine the level of service to the world when he begins to repay these karmas! At early soul ages we all get involved with some of this kind of experimentation, but it doesn't usually land on the front pages.

Richard Ramirez
Server/Server essence twin
Dominance—goal
Aggression—mode
Cynic—attitude
Arrogance—Chief feature
Instinctive Center/Intellectual Part
Infant, sixth level

CHAPTER ELEVEN
RESULTS

What is the result of having the Michael teaching intersecting with your life? Now that you have the basic information, where or what does it get you?

Throughout this introduction to the Michael system, self-knowledge has been touted as one important yield; tolerance, even agape, another. In an experiment to find if people did discover they understood themselves and tolerated others better, I asked a dozen people who have been involved with the teaching to tell me briefly what effect Michael has had on their lives.

I am allowing this Scholar to speak for many because she said succinctly what nearly everyone else also mentioned—in one way or another. "What has been most beneficial?" I asked.

"Two things. One: it was energizing, and many positive things happened during the first year. Michael was not the 'direct' cause, but things happen synergistically, always.

"Two: As a Scholar, I, of course, find all the specific labels and divisions interesting, but what is really important it that it is a device for understanding and tolerating the natural varieties people come in. It has enhanced my appreciation of others and increased my self-esteem."

A Sage told me, "I came out of a family where I was the only exalted role in a couple of generations and thus received much (successful) imprinting to not be conspicuous; I squished myself but managed to feel and appear the black sheep nevertheless. I am now learning how satisfying it is to stand out and be a little outrageous. I also no longer cringe from the public speaking aspects of my job, but enjoy them and the increase they bring to my business.

"The mildly eccentric grandmother I felt especially close to was an Old Soul; every other family member, late Baby to early Mature. That helped me understand some of the strong differences in attitude between myself and my family and drop many of my expectations of being 'understood', on my terms. Because I gained an overview on their perspectives and knew why they were unlikely to change, I became more sympathetic and less biased toward their viewpoints."

Another Sage told me, "The Michael information about Sages going naturally for what is fun was a lifesaver because I had, especially as a man, been secretly uneasy with myself for not thinking primarily in terms of productivity and usefulness as per my parental and good ol' American training. I now feel okay about judging things in terms of whether they are fun or not because judging in that fashion turns out to be typical Sage behavior and very probably a part of my road to 'enlightenment'."

"The most dramatic thing was finding out about my son," a go-getting Warrior told me. When he discovered his son was a seventh level Old Server with a goal of stagnation, he instantly got over years of upset that the son hadn't accomplished as much as expected. "Realizing he was essentially recovering from four exceedingly busy lifetimes in growth changed my life; my resentments and disappointments dropped away. I really love that kid, but had a hard time feeling or expressing it through all my aggravation.

"I now have a better understanding of why I do and don't do certain things. My goal is growth so there is always that excess enthusiasm for new things, not always accompanied by much discrimination. Knowing how high my 70% creative female energy is for a Warrior, has helped me understand why I am so disorganized right in the middle of being productivity oriented."

Another Warrior said she was "incredibly relieved" when she heard that Warriors actually need more sex than the other roles in order to balance themselves. From other spiritual practices, she'd gained the feeling her somewhat hyper-sexuality was a spiritual liability.

A father of four was buoyed to learn that his son, who had joined the Moonies and has been so far unavailable for communication for twelve months, would likely be coming back home before too long. "Michael explained that he was a Mature Priest looking for intensity, rapture and ecstasy within this group, but that as a Mature Soul he'd outgrow the Moonie's rigidity and find a way out. He told me the group contains mostly Baby Souls who buy the black and white, right and wrong principles laid down by Reverend Moon. Michael reminded me to be especially compassionate to my son when he returns because leaving a closely knit group, no matter how restrictive, can be more difficult than separating oneself from a decaying love affair, since the patterns of dependence and interdependence are more complicated in a group. I find myself much more peaceful about this situation now, and I don't think I'll be so inclined to wring his neck when he does finally appear. I have also stopped blaming myself; he's the one who chose this adventure."

A King I asked to describe how the teaching has been valuable began, "It's a good starting point for knowing why others don't think like I do. Knowing about others' soul ages is useful because I'm more conscious of my inability to twist them around, hoping to grow them quickly to my more 'reasonable' point of view.

"I've noticed a tendency in this teaching for people coming in to get very ego-involved about their soul age, whether 'impressively' high or 'embarassingly' low. However after being involved in the teaching for a while, this seems to mellow out.

"I like the potential for going from negative to positive on the overleaves. When I notice my chief feature, impatience, has kicked up and is driving me into a howling intolerance—which always feels uncomfortable—I have learned to breathe, ask myself if it does me any good to hang on, and if not let it go.

"I find the positive pole of my skeptic overleaf useful. It encourages me to check things out thoroughly, to think and evaluate, and to look for patterns. I like this, though the negative pole can make me a paranoid recluse relatively quickly. I am better than ever at avoiding this pitfall now."

A daring Scholar told me, "When I left my husband of 17 years for a woman, it was as much a suprise to me as a shock to the neighborhood—even though I felt it the right thing to do. Knowing my lover and I are essence twins, that she is at the eccentric fifth level experimenting with lifestyles outside the mainstream and that I, in a sixth level life, had a lot of karma to complete with my ex-husband, helped flesh out the circumstances surrounding this rather sudden change."

I heard from a Server who came from a very wealthy family which now shuns him due to a certain lack of ambition and competiveness: "Learning my mother, father and two brothers are all early Young Souls at the height of power and ambition helped me realize that however much I kicked myself to perform, it wasn't going to be enough to please them. I get excited about save-the-world causes, not about making more money. I am now guiltlessly putting my energy into environmental issues."

A Michael student who, with her daughter, shares a house with another mother and daughter, told me, "The other kid infuriated me so much I had thoughts about strangling her. I didn't enjoy feeling that way, but couldn't get a handle on what provoked me so much; the child was certainly nice enough and polite and cute and smart enough. She never really did anything provocative.

"Michael said the girl was a seventh level Young Scholar with a very heavy case of (seventh level) complacent know-it-all behavior, particularly obnoxious to Sages—me and my daughter—because of our love of disseminating information. This girl would take nothing we had to offer. I rather enjoy watching her run through her intellectually arrogant routines now that Michael pinned it down enough so that all my buttons aren't being pushed."

A sparkly Priest who learned she was in dominance said it helped her to accept her natural desire and ability to lead which she, as a woman raised in the 1940's, had mixed feelings about expressing. "It also helped explain the intensity of the battles in my family while I was growing up because my mom, dad, and myself were all in dominance! And all guarding our territories!!"

A mother of four grown children said she felt much more comfortable with the son she never seemed to reach or be able to affect. "I thought kids could grow in any direction if properly nurtured and loved; give them a good self-concept and watch them thrive. My son is at sixth level Mature, handling an incredible, nearly stupefying load of karma while being a not so charming cynic in power mode. Before I was bewildered as to why anyone would live life as he does or choose the attitudes he displays. I now have compassion for him, and that is quite a relief."

A friend who is an Artisan says Michael has helped her to accept herself better. "I understand why I am so independent; I'm better able to accept my own nature. I recognize my creativity is who I am to a very great extent. Staying home, creating, without nagging myself to socialize more is a treat I've been able to give myself.

"Knowing my goal is submission made me aware of why I have a pattern of subservience—and it helped me

135

accept and enjoy the plus side of submission which is my devotional nature.

"Learning my soul age initially upset me because third level Old was not seventh and I felt pretty advanced spiritually; I'd certainly been on the path long and diligently. But now I feel more self-accepting myself and of my own doubts, dramas and machinations, which I'd previously tried to gunnysack. Acceptance of my soul age gave me the gumption to relax into and enjoy my truly introspective—third level—nature."

So, this is the sort of growth that ensues from involvement with Michael's teaching and perspectives. People actually do seem to create more tolerance for others, as well as more self-acceptance, knowledge and love. Worthy pursuits and goals—and not too hard to come by.

About the Author

For the last ten years she has worked in the healing arts as a vision therapist, a life/death transistions counselor and as a nutritional consultant. Joya has been channeling since the mid-seventies. When she was introduced to Michael in 1984, the process deepened immensely.

Joya is a co-author of *The Michael Game* and also writes a regular column called "Michael views the News" which appears in the quarterly, *The Michael Connection.* Joya currently divides her time between writing, channeling for private clients, gardening, life's routines, friends and fun.

She is available for both in-person and telephone channeling. If interested, write to her for details through Sage Publications.

New Michael Books

The following books may be ordered from your bookseller
or from Sage Publications.

Michael's Gemstone Dictionary
by Judithann H. David, channeled by JP Van Hulle
Energies and usage of gems and minerals according to the
Michael Teaching. Hundreds of precious and semi-precious gems
for memory, money, imagination, well-being etc. Find out why
you're attracted to your favorite stones. Fascinating and useful.
$8.95, Touchstone and the Michael Educational Foundation

The Michael Game
by the Michael Digest Group
This collection of articles explores such varying topics as :
"Whales and Dolphins as Sentient Beings"
"Confessions of a Walk-in"
"101 Questions to Ask a Channel"
$12.50, Warwick Press

Essence and Personality: The Michael Handbook
by Jose Stevens, Ph.D and Simon Warwick-Smith
This 350 page reference book entertains you while you
learn. It covers the grand scheme, soul ages and levels,
roles, overleaves, centering, body types and more—in depth.
$14.95, Warwick Press

The World According to Michael:
An Old Soul's Guide to the Universe
by Joya Pope
Delightful and succinct, it's a "Sage's" romp
through the basics of the Michael Teaching.
There is a lot of information here in a small, fun-to-read package.
For friends who are curious, it's the starter book of choice.
$8.95, Sage Publications

Books may be ordered from:
Sage Publications,
Box 6944,
San Mateo, CA 94403.
Add $1.00 per book, postage and handling.
In California, please add 6.5% tax.

Keep in Contact
with
The Michael Community
Subscribe *NOW* to
THE MICHAEL CONNECTION

- Featuring all the latest information about the Michael Teaching

- Focusing each issue on the basics of the Michael Teaching

- Resource directory for Michael teachers in the Bay Area

- Periodic reports from the Michael Community nationwide

- Articles of general interest to Michael students and all others in the metaphysical community

- Pictures, poetry, gossip, personal ads and much, much more...

The Michael Connection exists to support the network of Michael students by sharing information, activities and fun.
Join us and connect.

Please fill this out and mail to: The Michael Connection
P.O. Box 1873, Orinda, CA 94563

✀_____

❑ **Subscription.** Please mail the next 4 issues (1 year) to me at my very own Physical Plane address for only $15.

❑ **Back Issues.** Please send me back issues featuring the following roles (Circle each you wish to have sent): **Warriors Artisans Servers Scholars Sages Priests Kings** I have enclosed $4 for each issue.

❑ **Advertising.** I'd love to enjoy patronage from the Michael community. Please let me know how.

Name:_____**Phone:**_____

Address: _____

City/State/Zip: _____
Please make checks payable to: The Michael Connection